CW00546254

Loafing Around

making great bread at home

J. D. Vincent

Loafing Around — *making great bread at home*

Published by *Blashford Books*

First published 2015

ISBN 978-0-9934317-0-8

www.loafingaround.co.uk

Preface

For millennia, across much of the world, bread, of one sort or another, has been a critical staple. It may not hold quite such a position of importance today, but great bread, from the artisan baker, where the dough contains only wholesome ingredients, treated with respect and allowed the time for a full fermentation to develop the texture and flavour, remains one of life's great pleasures.

As a keen cook, I have been making bread for a long time, but in recent years became increasingly aware of the deficiencies of mass produced bread and dissatisfied with the products offered by the local supermarkets and bakeries. Although not the staple it once was, in that one can now live without it, we still consume vast quantities of bread in this country, and, sadly, the majority of it is a grossly inferior product. Our bread has been adulterated with arguably unnecessary ingredients, denied the time to develop naturally with a good fermentation, and poorly baked, resulting in bread with lacklustre crust and doughy interior, lacking the aroma and flavour of proper bread. With no artisan baker on our doorstep who could satisfy my craving for real bread, I set about developing the knowledge and skills needed to create such bread at home. One day I took this a step further, and made the decision that we would no longer buy bread from the supermarket or mediocre bakeries.

I soon realised that I would need to expand my repertoire somewhat. Whilst I had previously made a range of breads, from crusty white batons to rye sourdough, these were more occasional bakes, and now all of our bread needs would have to be produced at home. This included sorts of bread that I would not normally have baked, such as the sliced loaf that lives in the freezer, to be toasted on demand. So, I began to experiment. This book started merely as jottings in my recipe notebook, recording formulae that worked well for me. It took another step forward when I typed up a series of recipes and instructions on how to develop and maintain a sourdough culture for a baking session with friends. As the notes expanded, it was not long before the inevitable conclusion was reached that there was a book in the making.

In this book, as well as sharing my favourite bread recipes, I hope to show how easily great bread can be made at home. Whilst an amateur, such as myself, might never acquire the experience of the full time artisan baker, and has to work within certain limitations with respect to equipment, the bread produced can still be of the highest quality. The home baker even has some advantages; dough can be prepared gently by hand, giving it the full time and attention that it deserves, without many of the concerns that a commercial baker must undoubtedly contend with. Making great bread at home is not hard, but like any craft, a certain amount of knowledge and practice is needed to achieve a measure of mastery. There is no shortcut for practice, but I hope that this book might help to provide fellow home bakers with some of the knowledge and skills needed to develop their craft.

For further recipes and video tutorials visit: *www.loafingaround.co.uk*

Contents

Index of recipes

Conversions

°C	°F	Gas mark
190	374	5
200	392	6
210	410	6½
220	428	7
230	446	8
240	464	9
250	482	9½

cup	grams flour
¼	35
⅓	47
½	70
⅔	93
¾	105
1	140

grams	ounces
25	0.9
28	1.0
50	1.8
75	2.7
100	3.5
150	5.3
200	7.1
250	8.8
300	10.6
350	12.4
400	14.1
450	15.9
500	17.6

measure	ingredient	approximate weight in grams
teaspoon	yeast	3
½ teaspoon	yeast	1.5
¼ teaspoon	yeast	0.75
⅛ teaspoon	yeast	0.38
teaspoon	ground spice	2
tablespoon	chopped herbs	6
teaspoon	baking soda	5.5
tablespoon	honey, malt, treacle, or molasses	21
tablespoon	olive oil	13

1. Introduction

Before proceeding to the usual sort of introductory material, I begin with a simple recipe to demonstrate just how easy it is to make great bread at home, and the flavour that comes from allowing time for nature to do its work and properly ferment the dough.

1.1 Ten minute bread

It is certainly true that good bread takes time, but for most of that time the dough is doing its own thing, developing and fermenting while the baker is free to do other things. Some breads need more effort and attention than others, but to show just how little effort one can put in and still enjoy great tasting bread I wanted to put this simplest of yeast leavened breads here in the introduction, and offer it somewhat by way of a challenge. Anyone can find the time to prepare this bread — it takes just a few minutes to weigh out and mix the ingredients, there is no kneading or hard work, the dough just sits somewhere at room temperature and ferments until the next day, when it is quickly formed up and baked. The high percentage of water leads to an open crumb with large holes, and the long fermentation gives the bread a chewy texture and good flavour. I hope it is enough to convince the reader of the benefits of home made bread and encourage further exploration of the techniques needed to prepare really great bread at home.

There are only four ingredients in this recipe — flour, water, salt, and yeast — all that is needed for good bread. For this recipe, use a strong bread flour and instant dried yeast — the sort commonly available from the supermarket in small sachets or pots.

Table 1.1: Ten minute bread

Ingredient	Weight (grams)
white wheat flour	300
water	225
salt	6
yeast	0.75 (¼ tsp)

Method

- Weigh all of the ingredients into a bowl and mix well.
- Cover with a cloth and leave to ferment for 12 to 18 hours.
- One hour before baking, heat the oven to 250°C, preferably with a baking stone — see Section 1.3 — or otherwise a heavy baking sheet on the middle shelf.
- When ready to bake, generously flour a peel or the reverse side of a baking sheet and gently turn the dough out of the bowl. It will be soft and sticky.

1

- Sprinkle with a little more flour, then gently form into shape. Divide the dough into smaller pieces, if desired, or bake in one large piece.
- Slide the dough onto the hot baking stone or sheet.
- Bake for around 15 minutes.
- Remove the bread from the oven and allow to cool on a wire rack.

Flour, water, yeast, and salt—all that is needed for good bread

Mix until fully combined

Mixed and ready to ferment

The dough after fermenting for 12 hours—risen and full of bubbles

Gently scoop out the soft dough so as not to deflate

Lightly flour the top before shaping

Divide and shape the dough

Freshly baked and cooling on a rack

The open crumb produced by the high moisture content and long fermentation

1.2   Home made bread

With bread so readily available from the supermarket or local bakeries, there are, perhaps, three good reasons to consider making it at home. The first is easy to explain. If I think of my favourite breads, they tend to be those we have found abroad: fougasse from Corsica; focaccia from Tuscany, rich in olive oil and topped with onions; and the dark ryes from my wife's home country of Finland. Although I have in the past bought plenty of it, I never crave a bread from our local supermarkets or bakeries. Whilst there are artisan bakers that no doubt produce excellent bread, we do not have one nearby. If I want great bread at home, I have to bake it myself.

The second reason is control of ingredients and method. Commercial bread is, more often than not, made with various ingredients that I do not want in my bread and would never consider adding to one of my recipes. These may be included for preservative properties or to counter shortcuts in a manufacturing process that produces bread without the full fermentation of a more traditional method. I want real bread; bread made with flour, water, salt, and yeast, as the primary ingredients, mixed and kneaded gently, preferably by hand, and allowed to develop naturally for a full flavour and good texture and crust. By making bread at home, one has the opportunity to prepare a wholesome product and in whatever style one prefers.

The third reason is that making bread from scratch is, for me, an enjoyable and therapeutic process. I have been a keen cook for many years, but of all the things that I prepare in the kitchen, there are few that I enjoy as much as making bread. There is something endlessly fascinating about the transformation of the simplest of ingredients into quite different breads with only small variations in the proportions and method of preparation. Real bread has been largely replaced by an inferior substitute, but I have found that I can produce with great success those breads that I want to eat at home, and much pleasure can be derived from their preparation.

Making bread at home does not require too much equipment, nor expensive ingredients. Some understanding and practice are needed to develop really great bread, but that is what this book aims to share. Once the basic techniques are acquired, it is not a hard or complex process. Good bread does take time, but it does not take much effort on the part of the baker. Baking may be a weekend activity for many, but there are ways to have homemade bread available throughout the week when time might otherwise be short. Sliced loaves can be frozen so that toast is available whenever it is needed, and although I am not generally a fan of the freezer, it works well for sliced bread. Aside from freezing, there are quick and easy ways to prepare bread—the ten minute recipe at the start of this chapter is one example, and the flatbreads of Chapter 6 can be made in a large batch and baked as needed over the course of several days, during which time the dough will improve in flavour.

1.3 Equipment

Making bread at home does not require much equipment, and none is particularly extravagant. Along with an area of worktop or a board on which dough may be worked, the essential items—most of which will already be available in the kitchen—include:

Mixing bowls and jugs At least one bowl is needed in which dough can be mixed and fermented. Various materials can be used—the traditional glazed earthenware, stainless steel, or food grade plastic. Dough can be fermented and folded in various plastic tubs if preferred, and, on a larger scale, one can buy stackable rectangular tubs made for the purpose. For just a few loaves at home, though, a good sized mixing bowl should suffice. Bowls need to be sufficient for the quantity of dough and allow enough space for this dough to rise during fermentation. Smaller bowls are useful for preferments. Jugs of various sizes are handy for liquid ingredients. A reasonably equipped kitchen should have all that is needed in this regard.

Kitchen scales Bread ingredients are usually weighed rather than measured by volume. Flour, in particular, can vary significantly in volume depending on how loosely it is packed. A good set of digital scales, with a tare function, is ideal for weighing ingredients and scaling portions of dough. Although not expensive, it is best if such scales are accurate and repeatable to 1 g. Most kitchen scales will be perfectly adequate for the weighing out of flour, water, and such, but scales can vary somewhat in performance when weighing small amounts such as a few grams of salt or yeast.

Dough scraper A simple plastic dough scraper is, perhaps, the most useful tool to have. I always have a few to hand. They are cheap, and all that one needs for mixing dough, helping to fold wet doughs, removing preferments and dough from tubs and bowls, scraping up excess dough and flour from the worktop, dividing dough into portions, and so on. Along with the plastic dough scrapers, I also have a straight edged metal scraper, which is handy for dividing dough and scraping the worktop after use, but this is by no means essential, and one must be careful that any such tool does not scratch and damage the work surface.

Baking stone A baking stone is not essential, in the sense that one can bake bread without it. It is, though, in my view, such a great benefit that I include it in this list. A baking stone is arguably essential for achieving a good crust when making pizza in a domestic oven, and greatly beneficial for baking all manner of breads. I have two, made essentially from clay fired to a high temperature, and I would not be without them. I prefer a large rectangular sheet that more or less fills the oven shelf rather than the smaller round sorts that are often sold as pizza stones.

Baking sheets One or more baking sheets are useful for laying out shaped bread to prove. One can bake on the sheets if a baking stone is not available, or use the reverse side of the sheet much as one would use a peel, for loading loaves into the oven.

Cooling rack To prevent the crust from softening too much from the residual steam in the loaf, one or more cooling racks are useful.

Tea towel A tea towel is handy for covering bowls of dough during fermentation, floured for use as a couche on which baguettes and similar may be placed to prove, wrapping tortillas and similar breads whilst still warm to help keep them soft, and wrapping other bread products once baked and fully cooled. I prefer a natural linen tea towel but have used cotton also for many years. I now have half a dozen that I use only in bread baking, so that they are never washed with detergent; mostly I give them a quick shake outside to get rid of any excess flour or crumbs.

Sharp blade A sharp blade is useful for slashing the dough before baking, allowing it to expand properly when baked, as well as providing a decorative finish to a loaf, and, when properly done, preventing *ad hoc* bursting of the crust. One can procure a specific tool for the job, known as a *lame*, which is typically a handle that holds a razor blade, often in a curved position, and sometimes with a cover of some sort so that it may be safely stored in a drawer. With due care, one can use a razor blade without a handle, which is what I usually do. A thin sharp kitchen knife can also serve fairly well, and, although it may not cut quite so cleanly, is probably the safest option.

There are, of course, various other pieces of equipment that one may wish to acquire; except for certain types of bread, such as those requiring bread forms or loaf tins, none is essential.

Stand mixer A robust stand mixer with a dough hook can be used to mix and knead bread dough, taking much of the effort out of the job. I sometimes use one for pizza dough and other flatbreads, but in general prefer to mix and knead by hand, and would certainly not invest in one for the primary purpose of making bread. If using a mixer, note that dough is generally mixed at low speed and kneaded at higher speed; refer to the manufacturer's instructions for appropriate settings for the model of mixer concerned.

Digital temperature probe One can readily bake by sight, touch, and smell, but a low cost temperature probe that can be inserted into a loaf to check the internal temperature is very useful, especially when trying a recipe for the first time, to verify that the bread is properly cooked through, and help determine appropriate timings for achieving the right bake in the future.

Large lidded jar For developing a sourdough culture a jar with a lid is needed. The required size depends on how much starter is maintained, and one must allow enough space for the starter to expand by, perhaps, three times in volume when refreshed. Food grade plastic is acceptable, as is glass. I use one litre kilner jars, as I usually have a few of those to hand.

Bread forms Sourdough loaves are generally proved in some sort of bread form — often known by the French or German terms *banneton* or *brotform*. These are baskets, typically of cane, and sometimes with a cloth liner, which hold the dough in shape during the long prove time of sourdough bread. They are available in a range of sizes and shapes. The most common is, perhaps, the round form, which is ideal if using a Dutch oven or baking dome — see below — but others include long, thin, forms for batons, and various ovals. When starting out, perhaps begin as I did, with a couple of round bannetons sized for 500 g or 1 kg loaves.

Loaf tins The so-called hearth breads are shaped by hand and proved on trays or in bread forms, but to make something convenient for the toaster, a loaf tin is needed. I prefer a 2 lb loaf tin, which gives a decent sized loaf, perfect for slicing for toast. Loaf tins can be fairly cheap, but it is worth investing in a good quality product that will last a long time and, perhaps more importantly, from which the loaves can be readily released.

Measuring spoons Although most ingredients are weighed, and all the recipes in this book provide weights, those for yeast are rather small in the sort of amounts needed for home baking. Thus it is handy to have a set of small measuring spoons, particularly covering the ⅛, ¼, and ½ teaspoon range. See Section 1.4.3 regarding conversions for salt and yeast.

Rolling pin For flatbreads such as pitta, naan, pizza, and so on, as well as for various unleavened breads, a rolling pin is useful. Such breads are often pressed and slapped into shape, but this takes practice, and a rolling pin is certainly handy. I favour a large, plain, pin, of beech, without the sculpted handles that are rather more common.

Cutters Round cutters, either smooth or fluted, are useful for stamping out savoury or sweet scones, although a glass of a suitable size works well enough as a substitute.

Tortilla press A tortilla press — see Section 2.2 for illustration — is a fairly inexpensive gadget consisting of two round plates, hinged at one side and with a short lever on the opposite side. Balls of dough are placed between the plates, and the press used to form tortillas and other similar breads, such as roti. These can, of course, be pressed or rolled out, but if making regularly or in large quantities, a press may be a handy tool.

Dough whisk A tool often known as a Danish dough whisk may be handy for mixing, particularly of preferments and doughs with a lot of water. The shape is quite effective for mixing without getting too clogged up, where spoons and forks are not really a good choice. They come in different sizes, and I use one from time to time, but generally a dough scraper is quite effective for most mixing purposes.

Couche cloth A couche is a length of fabric on which various breads, especially baguettes, are placed to prove. The cloth is folded between the individual loaves to keep them separate. For two or three batons that one might make at home, a linen tea towel is quite effective, but couche cloth intended for the purpose can be bought. This is typically a natural linen of a rather heavy gauge and often available by the metre. It is a good idea to have something that is specifically reserved for bread making purposes. I keep both a length of couche cloth and half a dozen linen tea towels to hand.

Baking dome A baking dome of some sort appears to be quite popular amongst bread enthusiasts. They can be made for the purpose from clay, the same material as often used for baking stones, or one can use a heavy gauge cast iron casserole, sometimes known as a Dutch oven. The baking dome or Dutch oven is preheated in a hot oven before the bread is added. The enclosed environment retains the steam released from dough as it bakes, keeping a moist environment that is beneficial for the development of the bread. The lid is removed for the latter portion of the bake to allow the crust to brown and crisp properly. I have a *La Cloche* baking dome, and many regard this as a useful piece of equipment for achieving a certain style of bread. It is somewhat limited, of course, in size and shape, and is relatively expensive. Whilst I consider a baking stone to be an almost essential item for various sorts of bread, a baking dome or Dutch oven is something that one might consider if one becomes sufficiently enthusiastic about baking to justify the cost.

Peels and flipping boards Peels come in various shapes and sizes, small sorts of which are useful in the kitchen for getting bread on and off of a hot baking stone or baking sheet. A thin peel is especially useful for pizza which is rather tricky to handle otherwise. A flipping board, or planchette à pain as it may be known, is similar, being a narrow length of wood used primarily for transferring baguettes from couche cloth to a peel for loading into the oven, or can be used to load them directly. Of rather more importance to the larger scale baking operation, in the absence of a peel, one can make do with the reverse side of a baking sheet, but having the right tool for job might be helpful. I make regular use of a pizza peel, a flipping board, and a wider wooden peel, for handling various sorts of bread.

Bread board and knife It goes without saying that something with which to slice the bread is quite useful. A good quality serrated bread knife, along with a suitable ceramic sharpener, are well worth investing in, especially if slicing bread for the toaster. Keeping the knife sharp makes all the difference.

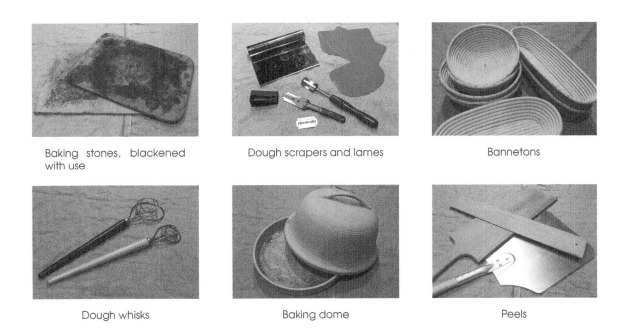

| Baking stones, blackened with use | Dough scrapers and lames | Bannetons |
| Dough whisks | Baking dome | Peels |

1.4 Concerning the recipes

The recipes included in this book are based on those that I make at home, recipes developed to replace any need I might have for supermarket bread products. This book is not, though, so much about the recipes as it is about the principles. Once the techniques are acquired, and an understanding gained of the effect of different ingredients and suitable proportions, one can readily put together a recipe to achieve whatever bread one has in mind. The recipes are sized to suit the home baker making one or two loaves at a time. I generally make them in the sizes listed or double the quantities.

Recipes are described in terms of weight of ingredients in grams. Even for those who might otherwise prefer imperial measures, grams are arguably rather more convenient for bread making purposes. Weighing ingredients is generally more accurate than using volume measures and it is very easy with a modern digital kitchen scale to weigh out all of the ingredients, including liquids.

Provided alongside the weights for the suggested batch size is the same recipe expressed in what is known as the *baker's percentage*. This is the best way to formulate a recipe and to compare different recipes. It is not complicated once the general principle is understood, but the totally maths shy can, by all means, entirely ignore that column of the recipe table.

The baker's percentage sets the total flour content to 100% and describes all other ingredients in proportion to the flour. When talking about the hydration of a dough, that is, the water content, one is generally talking in terms of the baker's percentage, where the water content typically ranges from around 50% for a dry dough to 80% for a very wet dough. These values are relative to the flour, so that, by weight, a 70% dough has 70 g water for every 100 g of flour. One can readily convert a recipe presented in weights to baker's percentage and *vice versa*.

1.4.1 Converting from weights to baker's percentage

Consider the recipe for the ten minute bread of Section 1.1, replicated in the table below. To convert to baker's percentage, one must merely determine an amount by which all of the weights must be divided:

$$divisor = \frac{total\ flour\ weight}{100}$$

For this example, the total flour weight is 300, so the divisor is $300/100 = 3$. Divide all of the quantities by this amount to calculate the percentages.

Ingredient	g	conversion to percentages
white wheat flour	300	300 / 3 = 100
water	225	225 / 3 = 75
salt	6	6 / 3 = 2
yeast	0.75	0.75 / 3 = 0.25

Many recipes call for several sorts of flours. The basic white dough of Section 5.1, for example, includes both white wheat flour and an amount of wholemeal rye. In such cases, converting to baker's percentage simply involves adding all of the flour weights, as illustrated below:

$$divisor = \frac{total\ flour\ weight}{100} = \frac{495 + 55}{100} = 5.5$$

Ingredient	g	conversion to percentages
white wheat flour	495	495 / 5.5 = 90
wholemeal rye flour	55	55 / 5.5 = 10
water	385	385 / 5.5 = 70
salt	11	11 / 5.5 = 2
yeast	4.1	4.1 / 5.5 = 0.75

Finally, there are recipes where ingredients are divided into a preferment or starter — see Chapters 7 and 8 respectively — and the main dough. Such recipes may be presented in various ways; in this book, the table is divided into three sections — one for the preferment or starter, one for the main dough, and then one for the overall formula, so that the total hydration and other ingredient proportions are clear.

1.4.2 Using baker's percentage to determine weights for a batch of dough

The purpose of the baker's percentage is to enable different formulations to be readily compared regardless of batch size. When working on a new recipe, it is in terms of percentages that one would tend to think. To go from these percentages to the required weights of the ingredients, the process above must be reversed. Consider the first example used above, for the ten minute bread, this time scaling from percentages to weights to provide a given batch size. To do so, one calculates a multiplier as follows:

$$multiplier = \frac{desired\,dough\,weight}{sum\,of\,percentages}$$

In each recipe, I include the sum of the percentages of each ingredient alongside the total weight for the suggested batch size. For the example below, let's say that we want three batons, each scaled at 250 g, thus requiring 750 g of dough; the multiplier is given by:

$$multiplier = \frac{750}{100 + 75 + 2 + 0.25} = \frac{750}{177.25} \approx 4.23$$

Each percentage in the recipe is multiplied by this multiplier to determine the required weight to achieve the desired batch size. The results are rounded to sensible figures — all but the yeast to the nearest gram, and the yeast to the nearest tenth of a gram. The process is identical, whether preferments are involved or not; simply divide the desired batch size by the quoted percentage sum to determine the multiplier to apply to each ingredient in the table.

Ingredient	%	conversion to weights
white wheat flour	100	100×4.23 = 423
water	75	75×4.23 = 317
salt	2	2×4.23 = 8
yeast	0.25	0.25×4.23 = 1.1

1.4.3   Concerns when baking in small batches

The batches of dough that one might prepare at home are fairly small, requiring a degree of care with measures. General kitchen scales should be entirely adequate for measuring weights of flour and water. In any event, the baker must use a certain amount of judgement in regard to the required amount of water to produce dough of the desired properties. For the salt, yeast, and perhaps some other ingredients, such as herbs and spices, kitchen scales may not be sufficiently accurate and/or repeatable for the small amounts involved. Ideally, a set of digital kitchen scales would enable repeatable measurement to the nearest gram, which is probably sufficient for measuring the salt content. If the scales are felt to be less accurate or repeatable than that, either some specialist scales are needed, or, more practically, the home baker may turn to measuring spoons for an approximation.

Salt is rather variable in grain size, so it is not possible to state what the weight of a teaspoon of salt might be. The fine grained sea salt that I am currently using for baking weighs, more or less, 5 g per teaspoon, whereas the coarse salt I use for other culinary purposes weighs only 3 g per teaspoon. One can determine a suitable conversion by weighing out, say, 10 or 20 teaspoons or so of salt to determine the typical weight of one teaspoon for the particular salt being used.

Similarly for the yeast, which one often needs to measure in parts of a gram. I use instant dried yeast in this book, for which I adopt an approximate conversion of 3 g per teaspoon. Thus, for the ten minute bread of Section 1.1, which calls for 0.75 g of yeast, I use ¼ of a teaspoon. Measuring spoons of ⅛, ¼, and ½ teaspoon are useful for this purpose.

1.5   Organisation of this book

Cookery books tend to focus on recipes, but, with bread in particular, the recipes are, in some ways, inconsequential. They are not, after all, overly complicated; some contain only the four basic ingredients of flour, water, salt, and yeast, and the latter are in predictable quantities, leaving only the ratio of flour to water as the key variable. More important, then, is to convey the methods and techniques involved, and impart an understanding of the effects of various ingredients on the finished product, thus enabling the reader to construct any bread of choice from basic principles. So, along with a range of recipes that provide us with home made replacements for anything we might otherwise have bought, the book is organised so that, hopefully, someone new to baking bread can work through it and acquire the knowledge and skills needed to create new recipes with confidence.

The chapters follow a natural progression, starting in Chapter 2 with unleavened bread, that is, bread without a raising agent. This is followed in Chapter 3 with breads leavened with baking soda, from classic soda bread to various scones. Although we make these sorts of bread from time to time, it is those leavened with yeast and allowed a proper fermentation that we make most often, and they therefore form the bulk of this book. The fermentation involved when yeast is used to raise bread brings much benefit, not only in terms of flavour and texture, but significantly in terms of digestibility. Unleavened bread and soda bread are technically straight forward, but working with yeast is a little more involved. The technicalities are discussed in Chapter 4, along with illustrations of the techniques involved with working the dough, on which the rest of the book is based.

Chapter 5 begins with basic yeast breads, so-called straight doughs that can be prepared in one session, without preferments, which are used to provide additional strength and flavour to the bread but take time to develop. Chapter 6 follows with doughs for various flatbreads. These are also straight doughs, and can be baked the same day as the dough is prepared, but also refrigerated and baked over the course of several days. This slow development in the refrigerator provides much improved flavour, much like using a preferment. Chapter 7 covers breads made with preferments, where part of the flour is fermented for a lengthy period before adding to the main dough. Chapter 8 then progresses from preferments made from baker's yeast to those made from the wild yeasts of a sourdough culture. Sourdough has a reputation for being complicated, but the transition from the breads of the preceding chapter is not at all so. A method is described for developing and maintaining a sourdough culture, then recipes provided that use this culture to create breads leavened entirely with natural yeasts.

One method, many doughs Different bakers no doubt have their own particular method for developing a dough. That same method, though, can be applied, with but minor variations, to a wide range of doughs. There is little difference between making a white bread or a wholemeal bread; the method can be identical, but the flours used and, most likely, the amount of water, will vary. Thus, at the start of Chapter 5, the general method for developing a straight dough is covered in detail. This same method is then applied throughout much of the rest of the book. Rather than repeat the method in detail for each recipe, only any important points of variation are noted. The method is developed further in chapters 7 and 8 for using a preferment and a sourdough culture respectively.

One dough, many breads I often have a particular purpose in mind with a given dough. For example, I usually use the half wholemeal recipe of Section 5.2 to make a traditional shaped loaf for slicing for toast, baking it in a loaf tin. However, the dough could equally be shaped into rolls, or baked as a hearth bread of some sort. Sometimes a recipe might be varied slightly depending on the form, perhaps adjusting the hydration, but generally each dough can be used in various ways to make a range of bread forms. By adding other ingredients, from herbs and spices, to fruits, nuts, seeds, and grains, or olives, cheese, onions, and so on, one can create, with a small number of basic doughs, a practically unlimited variety of breads. Each recipe table includes a column for notes, where the reader may make annotations or amendments to suit specific flours or tastes.

2. Unleavened bread

It is not known for certain when leavened bread came to be produced on a regular basis, but for millennia the actions of wild yeasts, occurring naturally on grains and otherwise abounding in the environment, have been exploited to produce bread with a lighter and more pleasing texture. Early breads, though, were unleavened, being little more than a coarse meal, mixed with a little water, and perhaps cooked on a hot stone. Whilst we encounter unleavened breads infrequently here, they have remained an important part of the cuisine and tradition of many cultures, notably those from the Middle East and other regions of Asia, and also as an element of religious observance, amongst, for example, Jewish and Christian communities.

Although there are many sorts of unleavened bread, their preparation is similar. The doughs are quick to make, but those containing wheat benefit from a period of relaxation after kneading, before rolling and cooking. They can be cooked on a baking stone or heavy baking sheet in a hot oven, or on a griddle pan. Portions of dough may be shaped and slapped between hands, rolled out, or formed with the help of a tortilla press or similar gadget. Those skilled in the art can produce perfectly formed circles of thin dough in moments, but even without such skills one can readily produce quick and tasty unleavened bread. The bread can be crisp and cracker like, especially if baked in the oven, or soft and flexible, particularly if oil has been added to the dough and the hot breads wrapped in cloth as soon as they are cooked, where the residual steam will help to prevent a dry crust from forming.

2.1 White wheat and olive oil flatbreads

This flatbread is somewhat typical of a wide range of sorts produced throughout the Middle East, and is the ideal accompaniment to hummus and other such dishes. A white wheat flour is combined with water, olive oil, and a little salt, and kneaded to form an elastic dough. After resting, this can be rolled out thinly and baked, preferably on a baking stone, but otherwise on a heavy baking sheet, in a hot oven. I like to achieve a fairly crisp result, but baking at a lower temperature will help produce a softer bread, as will wrapping the just cooked bread in a cloth. The flatbreads can be reheated, if desired, either in the oven or popped briefly into a suitable toaster.

Method

- Heat the oven to 250°C, preferably with a baking stone, or otherwise a heavy baking sheet.
- Place all of the ingredients in a bowl.
- Mix until fully combined.
- Tip out onto the worktop and knead until smooth and elastic; about ten minutes. For

kneading techniques, see Section 4.9.

- Return to the bowl, cover with a cloth, and leave to rest for 15 minutes or so to allow the dough to relax.
- Divide the dough into golf ball sized portions.
- Lightly dust the worktop with flour and roll out each ball to a thin sheet.
- Dock the dough in several places, that is, pierce through with a knife or fork, to prevent excessive puffing of the flatbreads.
- Transfer the flattened dough, in batches, to the baking stone or tray, and cook for three or four minutes until golden brown.

Table 2.1: White wheat and olive oil flatbread

Ingredient	g	%	Notes
white wheat flour	250	100	
water	125	50	
olive oil	25	10	
salt	5	2	
batch size (6 to 8 flatbreads)	405	162	

2.2 Corn tortillas

The sort of tortillas one finds most often in the supermarket are made largely or entirely from wheat flour and leavened with some sort of baking powder. I rather prefer such bread to be leavened with yeast — see Section 6.3. Although wheat versions now dominate, their origin lies in unleavened breads made from corn — maize — meal. These are quite different from wheat tortillas, and not readily available here. Those labelled as corn tortillas often include some wheat flour and can have a rather low proportion of corn. The corn in question is field corn and the flour to look out for is known as *masa harina*. This has been processed by liming the kernels — a treatment known a nixtamalisation. This is done to help remove the tough outer skin of the kernels and has the effect of making the nutrients in the corn more readily available. Finely ground, this flour can be quickly turned into a dough from which a corn tortilla may be produced, by simply mixing with water and a pinch of salt. Other sorts of maize flour are available, but do not work nearly so well as that specifically intended for the purpose.

The tortillas may be rolled or pressed into thin discs; using a tortilla press makes the process quick and easy. This inexpensive piece of equipment typically consists of two cast metal plates, hinged on one side, and with a lever on the other side that is used to press the two plates together. A couple of sheets of plastic film, such as from a food bag, are ideally placed on the plates, small balls of dough placed between them, and the dough pressed to

White wheat and olive oil flatbreads

the desired thickness. No oil should be needed in the process. Alternatively, one can place the ball between two layers of plastic on the worktop, and use the base of a heavy pan to press the dough.

Table 2.2: Corn tortillas

Ingredient	g	%	Notes
masa harina (corn meal)	200	100	
water	250	125	
salt	4	2	
batch size (8 to 10 tortillas)	454	227	

Method

- Place the corn meal and salt in a bowl and add around three quarters of the water.
- Mix well, adding further water until a smooth dough is formed.
- Allow to stand for ten minutes, then form into balls of around golf ball size.
- Press or roll into thin rounds.

- Cook on a moderately hot griddle pan for a minute or so on each side, turning as the edges begin to curl.
- Wrap the hot tortillas in a cloth to keep them warm and soft.

Tortilla press and corn tortillas from yellow and blue corn

2.3 Wholemeal roti

Roti is an unleavened bread, typically made from a wholemeal flour. It is a staple of Indian cuisine, and widely known throughout South and South East Asia, as well as parts of Africa and the Caribbean. Some recipes add a little oil or other fat, which may help to keep them soft, but here I make them with just flour, water, and salt. Traditionally, the roti are cooked on a pan known as a tawa, but a heavy griddle pan can be used. With due care, they may be finished by exposing to searing direct heat, such as from a gas or electric ring, whereupon the roti scorch a little

Roti puffing up in a hot flame

and puff up, as the steam inside forces the outer layers of crust to separate.

Table 2.3: Wholemeal roti

Ingredient	g	%	Notes
wholemeal wheat flour	250	100	
water	158	63	
salt	5	2	
batch size (8 to 10 roti)	*413*	*165*	

Wholemeal roti

Method

- Place all of the ingredients in a bowl.
- Mix until fully combined.
- Tip out onto the worktop and knead until smooth and elastic; about ten minutes.
- Return to the bowl, cover with a cloth, and leave to rest for 15 minutes or so to allow the dough to relax.

- Divide the dough into golf ball sized portions.
- Lightly dust the worktop with flour — white flour will work better than wholemeal for this purpose — and roll out each ball to a thin sheet.
- Cook on a hot griddle pan for around 20 seconds on each side, or a little longer if skipping the next step.
- Optionally, finish over direct heat, for just a few seconds on each side, until puffed.

3. Leavening with baking soda

The majority of our bread is leavened with some sort of yeast, whether a fast acting baker's yeast or the wild yeasts of a natural leaven. As well as leavening, that is, causing the bread to rise, the fermentation makes bread more digestible and brings much flavour. However, quick and tasty bread can be chemically leavened with baking soda — sodium bicarbonate — much the same as it is used in various cakes and batters. Sodium bicarbonate reacts in an acidic environment, releasing carbon dioxide. It is this release of gas that expands doughs to make them rise. The widespread use of such chemical leavening is relatively modern, soda bread becoming popular in the early 1800s, and having a traditional association with Ireland and Scotland.

It is important to distinguish between baking soda and baking powder — they are not the same thing, nor are they interchangeable without appropriate adaptations. Baking powders vary in composition, typically containing baking soda and one or more acidic components, such as cream of tartar. When the wet ingredients are added the reaction between the alkaline and acidic components is initiated. When using baking soda, recipes include one or more acidic ingredients, such as lemon juice or vinegar. For soda bread, the acidic component is traditionally derived from buttermilk, although yoghurt is a suitable alternative where buttermilk is not readily to hand.

Many recipes for scones, and some for soda bread, call for self raising flour. This is a plain flour — one of typically modest protein levels, as it is used for recipes where the development of the gluten in the flour is not helpful — with the addition of some sort of baking powder. Recipes often then require the addition of further baking powder to achieve the desired rise. Whilst the most common sort is made from white wheat, there are also wholemeal versions. I do not generally use self raising flours, preferring instead to use a plain flour and add my own, controlled, amount of baking powder or baking soda. I already have a lot of flours in the pantry and cannot see any good reason to keep a separate self raising flour. Different sources vary as to how much baking powder is needed to turn plain flour into the equivalent of self raising, but a good starting point might be one teaspoon, or 5.5 g, of baking powder to 150 g of flour.

When baking soda is used in making bread, the dough has to be prepared quickly, as it begins to release carbon dioxide as soon as the wet ingredients are added. There is no development of the gluten, as there is in yeast raised breads, thus there is little structure to the dough. The texture is typically fairly dense and the crumb even. For those that enjoy soda bread, as I do from time to time, the flavour of a loaf straight from the oven can be very good. Soda bread takes about five minutes to prepare and some 30 to 40 minutes to bake for a large loaf, and around 15 minutes if divided into smaller portions, so it is ideal when there is no time for leavening with yeast. Unlike yeasted breads, which are best left to cool thoroughly before slicing and warmed afterwards if desired, soda bread and scones are best eaten whilst still warm.

3.1 Soda bread

Soda bread can be prepared with any flour. As the gluten is not developed, protein levels are not important and one can readily experiment with different flours to achieve the desired flavour. Bear in mind, though, that different grains vary in how much moisture they absorb, and whole meal flours absorb more than white wheat flour, so adjust as necessary with a little milk or water. Although white flour can be used, I generally make soda bread with a 50 : 50 mix of white and wholemeal wheat flours. Spelt is another interesting option; its nutty flavour works really well in soda bread — see Section 3.2.2. Recipes often include some oats, either as meal in the dough, or as rolled oats sprinkled on top. Likewise, various seeds can be added according to taste.

3.1.1 Classic soda bread

This recipe produces a loaf with the distinctive taste and aroma of a classic soda bread. The traditional shape is rounded with a deep slash in a cross on top of the dough, which opens wide when baked.

Table 3.1: Soda bread

Ingredient	g	%	Notes
white wheat flour	250	50	
wholemeal wheat flour	250	50	
buttermilk (or yoghurt)	400	80	
baking soda	16.5 (3 *tsp*)	3.3	
salt	10	2	
batch size	*927*	*185.3*	

Method

- Place the flours, baking soda, and salt in a bowl and mix well.
- Add the buttermilk or yoghurt and mix to combine. If necessary add a little milk or water to form a somewhat sticky dough.
- Turn out onto a well floured surface and work gently, with floured hands if necessary, to bring the dough together.
- Shape into a slightly flattened ball and transfer to a well floured baking sheet.
- Sprinkle the top with a little flour then slash the dough, around one third to half way through, in a cross shape.
- Bake at 205°C for 35 to 45 minutes until nicely browned and sounding hollow if tapped on the bottom.
- Transfer to a wire rack to cool.

Soda bread

3.1.2 Soda griddle cakes

For this variant of soda bread, the dough is rolled and shaped into cakes of around 1 cm in thickness, which are cooked on a griddle rather than baked in the oven. I usually shape these into small rounds, but similar breads, known as farls, are formed into one round and scored into quarters.

Method

- Place the flour, baking soda, and salt in a bowl and mix well.
- Add the buttermilk or yoghurt and mix to combine. If necessary add a little milk or

water to form a somewhat sticky dough.

- Turn out onto a well floured surface and work gently, with floured hands if necessary, to bring the dough together.
- Pat or roll out the dough into four small rounds of around 1 cm in thickness.
- Cook in a heavy griddle pan over low to medium heat for around six minutes on each side, until golden brown and cooked through.
- Transfer to a wire rack to cool, or serve immediately.

Table 3.2: Soda griddle cakes

Ingredient	g	%	Notes
white wheat flour	175	100	
buttermilk (or yoghurt)	150	80	
baking soda	5.5 (1 *tsp*)	3.1	
salt	3.5	2	
batch size (four small griddle cakes)	*334*	*185.1*	

Griddle cakes

3.2 Scones

Scones are a form of soda bread that are typically rolled or patted out to a few centimetres in thickness and stamped with a round, often fluted, cutter. They can be prepared as a savoury, when they are bread like, or sweet, often with fruit, when they are almost cake like. Unlike soda bread, scones are enriched with fat, preferably butter. As they bake, the water content of the butter turns to steam, helping to raise the scones, producing a lighter and more flaky texture. The butter should be cold when preparing the dough, and can be grated into the flour or diced up and worked in by fingertip. If grated, the texture is more flaky and rustic than if rubbed into the flour.

The secret to good scones is, first, to get the quantities right, adjusting the liquid by feel to produce a slightly sticky dough, and then to handle this as little and as quickly as possible. Use only enough effort needed to bring the dough together, roll or pat out gently, and stamp out with care. Have the oven hot and ready to go, and get the scones in as soon as they are ready. Use plenty of flour on the work bench and well floured hands to prevent sticking, but be careful not to incorporate too much of this into the dough. I generally bring the dough together on an unfloured surface, then flour an area for rolling out.

3.2.1 Quick savoury scones

This recipe for a rustic savoury scone makes the ideal breakfast accompaniment, or quick bread in the evening when time is short, and is not unlike that which the Americans refer to as biscuits. It is an old recipe that my wife has used for many years, and calls for baking powder rather than baking soda. Thus, one can use milk or other liquid, rather than buttermilk or yoghurt. The dough is quite sticky, so best handled with well floured hands. The dough can be shaped in various ways; I like to form it into a rough square, then cut into four pieces with a dough scraper.

Method

- Place the flour, baking powder, and salt in a bowl and mix well.
- Grate the butter into the flour or cut the butter into small pieces and rub into the flour using fingertips until a coarse crumb is achieved.
- Add the milk and mix to combine, adding extra liquid if necessary to form a somewhat sticky dough.
- Turn out onto a well floured surface and, with well floured hands, pat into a rough square shape around 2.5 cm thick.
- Cut into four pieces and transfer to a baking sheet.
- If desired, brush the top with milk or beaten egg to glaze.
- Bake at 205°C for around 20 minutes until lightly golden on top.

- Serve immediately or transfer to a wire rack to cool.

Table 3.3: Savoury scones

Ingredient	g	%	Notes
white wheat flour	250	100	
butter	50	20	
milk	175	70	
baking powder	11 (2 tsp)	4.4	
salt	5	2	
batch size (4 large scones)	491	196.4	

Savoury scones

3.2.2 Cheese, herb, and spelt scones

Cheese scones promise much, but are often a little disappointing; they can turn out dry and lacking in flavour. This recipe, though, makes the most delicious savoury scones, with the buttermilk giving a light texture. I use a combination of white wheat flour and wholemeal spelt flour, the latter lending a nutty flavour to the scones. As cheese is added to the dough, one must be cautious with the level of added salt, which one might wish to vary according to the cheese used. I use a mature firm cheese for this recipe; cheddar is ideal, as is an aged Comteé or Gruyère. I add a little fresh rosemary to these scones, but by all means substitute other herbs if desired. Fresh herbs, though, are much to be preferred to the dried sort. The addition of a little mustard powder and paprika or cayenne pepper works well with the cheese, but can be omitted if preferred or other spices substituted.

Table 3.4: Cheese, herb, and spelt scones

Ingredient	g	%	Notes
white wheat flour	175	50	
wholemeal spelt flour	175	50	
butter	100	29	
buttermilk	250	71	
mature cheese	200	57	
chopped rosemary	6 (1 *tbsp*)	1.7	
mustard powder	1 (½ *tsp*)	0.3	
paprika or cayenne pepper	2 (1 *tsp*)	0.6	
baking soda	11 (2 *tsp*)	3.1	
salt	5	1.4	
batch size (approx. 12 scones)	925	264.2	

Method

- Place the dry ingredients — flours, rosemary, mustard powder, paprika or cayenne pepper, baking soda, and salt — in a bowl and mix well.
- Grate the butter into the flour or cut the butter into small pieces and rub into the flour using fingertips until a coarse crumb is achieved.
- Grate the cheese and add ¾ to the bowl, reserving the remainder for topping the scones.
- Add the buttermilk, and mix to combine. If necessary, add a little milk or water if too dry, or a little more flour if too wet. The dough should be somewhat sticky.
- Turn out onto a floured surface and work gently, with floured hands if necessary, just enough to bring the dough together to allow it to be rolled out.

- Sprinkle with more flour, if necessary, and gently pat and/or roll out the dough to a thickness of around 2.5 cm.
- Stamp out the scones with a cutter or the rim of a glass and transfer to a baking sheet, leaving plenty of space between them.
- Dust excess flour from the remaining dough and gently reform. Stamp out more scones, and repeat until all of the dough is used.
- Sprinkle the remaining cheese on top of the scones.
- Bake at 205°C for around 15 minutes until golden brown.
- Transfer to a wire rack to cool. Best served whilst still warm.

Cheese, herb, and spelt scones

3.2.3 Sweet scones for afternoon tea

Although this book is largely about savoury breads, I could not leave this section without a recipe for the sort of sweet scones that one might prepare for afternoon tea. The inclusion of fruit in the scone is a matter of personal preference and one might wish to prepare the dough in two batches, one with fruit and one without for those that prefer a plain scone. The fruit can be added directly to the dough, or it can, as suggested here, be soaked first, either overnight or just for an hour or two, to plump up. In this recipe, tea is used as the soaking liquor, which adds something to the flavour and seems entirely appropriate for a scone intended, after all, for afternoon tea.

Raisins or sultanas are the most commonly added fruits, but any of the candied, dried, or semi dried fruits can be used, such as cherries, dates, apricots, and citrus peel. Nuts and seeds can also be included, with walnuts being a particularly good candidate. Scones can also be flavoured with a variety of spices, such as cinnamon, cloves, allspice, or cardamom. Citrus zest can be added to the dough, or citrus juice used to soak the fruit. The humble scone offers, in fact, a rather wide range of possible flavours and textures to experiment with.

For my afternoon tea scone, I use sultanas soaked in Earl Grey tea. The tea has some citrus notes from bergamot oil, which are built upon here with a little orange zest. Like the previous recipe, baking soda and buttermilk give a light texture, but this time the dough is enriched with egg. The result is a light and flavoursome scone, perfect served with jam and clotted cream and, of course, a nice cup of tea.

Method

- Soak the fruit in the tea for a few hours or overnight.
- Place the dry ingredients — flour, sugar, baking soda, and salt — in a bowl and mix well.
- Grate the butter into the flour or cut the butter into small pieces and rub into the flour using fingertips until a coarse crumb is achieved.
- Beat the egg with the buttermilk and add to the flour.
- Add the fruit and soaking liquor, and the orange zest.
- Mix to combine. If necessary add a little milk or water to form a somewhat sticky dough.
- Turn out onto a floured surface and work gently, with floured hands if necessary, just enough to bring the dough together to allow it to be rolled out.
- Sprinkle with more flour, if necessary, and gently pat and/or roll out the dough to a thickness of around 2.5 cm.
- Stamp out the scones with a cutter or the rim of a glass and transfer to a baking sheet, leaving plenty of space between the scones.

- Dust excess flour from the remaining dough and gently reform. Stamp out more scones, and repeat until all of the dough is used.
- Brush with a little milk or beaten egg to glaze if desired.
- Bake at 205°C for 12 to 15 minutes, until golden brown.
- Transfer to a wire rack to cool. Best served whilst still warm.

Table 3.5: Sweet fruited scones

Ingredient	g	%	Notes
white wheat flour	250	100	
butter	50	20	
buttermilk	125	50	
sugar	40	16	
sultanas (or other dried fruit)	75	30	
strong tea	50	20	
orange zest	2 (1 tsp)	0.8	
egg	50 (1 medium)	20	
baking soda	11 (2 tsp)	4.4	
salt	1	0.4	
batch size (approx. 8 scones)	654	261.6	

Sweet scones

4.   Leavening with yeast

Most of our bread is leavened with yeast. Unlike our forebears, though, who would exploit
wild yeasts—such as we still do with sourdough cultures, Chapter 8—the majority of
modern bread is made with selected strains of yeast that provide for a rapid rise. A rapid
rise, though, is only good from the perspective of the mass production of an inferior product;
a more slowly developed dough will yield better bread with more flavour. However, there
is no reason why one cannot adopt a slower, more traditional, process and make fantastic
breads with baker's yeast; one simply has to reduce the amount used, eliminate extraneous
ingredients, and allow time for a proper fermentation.

Yeast serves the same purpose as the baking soda of the previous chapter, producing
carbon dioxide to raise the dough. There are two key differences, though, when leavening
with yeast. First, the process takes, under normal conditions, at least several hours, whereas
the carbon dioxide is released quickly when using baking soda. Second, one has the time to
develop the gluten in the dough, which provides the structure needed to more effectively trap
and hold the carbon dioxide, allowing the production of bread with a light, airy, texture.

Although making bread with yeast is not particularly complicated—after all, only four
main ingredients are involved—the underlying processes are not quite so straightforward.
To become comfortable with developing or adapting recipes and methods, one must appreci-
ate the effect that different ingredients and processes may have on the finished product, and
thus venture at least a little into the science of bread making. Whilst the commercial baker
may need to understand these matters in rather more depth and exert more control on the
process so that the outcomes are repeatable, in terms of both the qualities of the finished
product and how long each batch of bread takes from start to finish so that production may
be efficiently scheduled, the home baker has much less to worry about.

In this chapter, I have tried to distil the important points of making bread with yeast.
Subsequent chapters provide practical recipes for simple yeast breads (Chapter 5), flatbreads
(Chapter 6), breads with preferments (Chapter 7), and sourdough (Chapter 8). The reader
does not necessarily need to study the material in this chapter in great detail, but Section
4.9 may be particularly useful to those new to bread making as it describes techniques for
working with the dough, and Section 4.8, which outlines the general baking parameters
adopted for most of the subsequent recipes.

4.1   The basic process

The process of preparing a bread leavened with yeast may be broken down into various
stages, of which six are considered here for a straight dough, that is, a dough made without
a preferment. Preferments and sourdough cultures, both of which involve the fermentation
of a portion of the flour and water content of the recipe for some hours before adding to the
main dough ingredients, are considered in more detail in chapters 7 and 8 respectively.

1. Mixing of ingredients.

2. Development of gluten.

3. Bulk fermentation.

4. Dividing and shaping.

5. Final prove.

6. Scoring and baking.

Consider a basic yeast bread, such as that of Section 5.1. The mixing stage involves adding the required amounts of flour, water, salt, and yeast to a bowl or other vessel, and combining until a fairly homogeneous mass is produced. If using a mixer with a dough hook this is typically done at a low speed. Once mixed, the gluten in the dough is developed by kneading. By hand, kneading can be a fairly gentle process of stretching and folding the dough. If using a mixer, this stage is typically done at a higher speed. Kneading is complete when the desired elastic properties of the dough are achieved. The dough is then left to ferment for an hour or two. It is then divided into portions, if necessary, and shaped to suit the bread form being made. The shaped dough is left to prove until ready to bake, generally doubling in volume, to produce an airy texture. Finally, the dough is scored, if necessary, and baked. Some of the important aspects associated with each stage are discussed in more detail in the following sections.

4.2   Ingredients

Although commercial offerings may be adulterated with all manner of unnecessary ingredients, delicious artisan bread is made with few ingredients, often nothing more than flour, water, salt, and some sort of yeast. There is, though, a wide range of ingredients that may quite legitimately be included; these are used for their contributions to texture, flavour, and nutrition rather than as an aid to short-cut the fermentation process, artificially extend shelf life, or address some other perceived defect of a poor quality loaf.

4.2.1   Flour

Whilst flours can be produced from all manner of starchy plant material, such as the seeds of legumes and grasses, as well as tubers and roots, it is those produced from the grains of wheat and rye that are most often used in bread making. Wheat is the most important, and for good reason. Along with high yields of grains that are relatively easy to process, wheat contains good levels of the proteins needed to form light, airy, bread.

Flours milled from grain are available with varying proportions of the whole grain, which may be referred to as the extraction rate. Grains consist of three main parts: the bran, which is the outer coating; the germ, which is the embryo that, under suitable conditions, can sprout into new life; and the endosperm, the larger part of the grain, which provides the food source for the germinating embryo. Wholemeal flours, as the name implies, utilise the entire grain. White flours utilise around 70%, with brown flours somewhere between white and wholemeal. The germ in particular contains various vitamins and minerals that are lost in white flours. The popularity of breads produced from white flours led to the practice of routine fortification. Thus, flours are supplemented with calcium, iron, niacin (vitamin B3) and thiamin (vitamin B1). These are, at the time of writing, matters for the regulatory framework and not something over which the baker or consumer has any choice.

Wheat flours are readily available with various extraction rates. Others, such as rye and spelt, are more likely to be wholemeal, although more refined versions are available. In general, a white wheat flour is very useful, but for rye and spelt I most often use the wholemeal sorts. Unless one is deliberately trying to avoid using modern wheat, combining a certain amount of white wheat with wholemeal rye or spelt is a beneficial way of making a lighter blend of flours, as the wheat gives the best structure to the bread.

Wheat For wheat flour in particular, the protein content is an important consideration. Plain flour — also known as all purpose flour — might have around 9 to 11% protein, a bread flour might have around 11 to 13% and a strong bread flour from 13 to approaching 15%. Of the proteins in flour, two are of particular interest, gliadin and glutenin, which make up the majority of the protein in wheat flour. In the presence of water, these proteins can link to form gluten, which gives the dough its stretch and allows it to trap the carbon dioxide released by the yeast in order to raise the bread.

Glutenin and gliadin contribute different properties to the dough; the former is responsible for elasticity and the latter for extensibility. Elasticity is the property that allows the dough to be stretched without tearing. An elastic dough will tend to return to its original shape after stretching. Without elasticity, the gluten network could not expand to hold the carbon dioxide; the dough would tear and the gas escape. Extensibility is the property that allows the dough to be reshaped. Without extensibility, the dough could not expand to provide well risen bread. These two properties are somewhat opposed. A dough that is as elastic as possible — which is generally what is meant when talking about the strength of the dough — would be, for example, difficult to shape into baguettes or flatbreads that require a reasonable degree of extensibility. Thus, it is not simply a matter of selecting a high protein flour and working it to develop the gluten to its full potential. There can be such a thing as too much gluten development, or too much strength to the dough. Such a dough would not expand well during proving and during the bake. It is, therefore, a matter of balance, and of adjusting the formulation of the dough, and the method of working, to suit the bread being made. This will vary depending on the form of the bread; loaves shaped and baked on a sheet or baking stone — so-called hearth loaves — need more strength in the dough to hold their shape whilst proving and baking than those proved and baked in a pan.

I tend to use a strong bread flour, with a moderately high protein level, but it is a good idea to experiment with different flours from different brands. Locally produced flours are likely to be less strong than, say, the very strong imported Canadian wheat flours, and I do prefer a locally produced organic flour where possible. One can readily blend a strong flour with a softer flour to produce the right properties for the bread. If the bread holds its shape well but turns out on the dense side and with an overly chewy texture, one might look at softening the flour. Similarly, if the dough is difficult to stretch when shaping. Conversely, if the bread is easy to shape but tends to flatten, or if the rise is poor, then one might look to strengthening the flour blend. Naturally, there are many other factors that impinge on dough strength, such as the degree to which the gluten has been developed by kneading, mechanically or by hand, whether the dough is folded during fermentation, the length of fermentation, use of preferments, and so on; each of these factors will be treated in due course.

Rye After wheat flour, rye is the most important in bread making. Rye breads are particularly common through northern and eastern Europe, where the weather conditions are more favourable for growing rye than they are for wheat. Rye flour is high in protein, but whereas wheat flour has gliadin and glutenin in good balance, from a bread making perspective, rye has plenty of gliadin and low levels of glutenin. As a consequence, there is little gluten development in a dough made purely from rye.

Much of the structure of a rye bread is due to the carbohydrates known as pentosans, which rye has in much higher proportions than other flours. Rye can hold some gas, but has nothing like the capabilities of wheat in this regard. Pentosans absorb large amounts of water, much of which is retained during baking, so that rye bread tends to be moist and remain fresh for longer than wheat. Pure rye doughs require no kneading and one must be careful in the mixing also, as the pentosans are readily damaged, which can lead to a sticky dough.

Rye flour tends to be much higher in the enzyme amylase, so converts starch to sugar more rapidly than wheat flours, see Section 4.5. This results in more rapid fermentation, but as the starch is an important part of bread structure, too much enzyme activity can result in the degradation of the structure if allowed to over prove, resulting in a sticky crumb. Bread made with high proportions of rye flour is most often leavened with a sourdough culture — see Chapter 8 — the acidity of which helps to inhibit the activity of the amylase.

It should be evident that making a good wheat bread is rather easier than making a good rye bread. Nonetheless, rye breads can be especially flavoursome and they keep well, particularly when prepared with a sourdough culture. Rye breads tend to be quite dense unless mixed with a majority of wheat flour to provide the gluten network. A dense, strongly flavoured sourdough rye is, though, delicious, if one appreciates this sort of bread.

Spelt and other grains Although wheat and rye account for the vast majority of our bread, there are other grains that one might experiment with. The most common alternative is spelt, an ancient relative of common wheat that brings a wonderful nutty flavour to bread. It does contain the gluten forming proteins gliadin and glutenin, but in a higher ratio than wheat. Thus, spelt dough tends to be more extensible and less elastic than wheat dough and spelt bread tends to be more dense. Nonetheless, I like to use wholemeal spelt in various recipes, either on its own or in combination with white wheat flour. A number of other ancient grains may be found, including einkorn, emmer, and khorasan, although these are cultivated in relatively small quantities. A specific variety of khorasan is marketed under the trademark Kamut. Any of these flours, where available, can be used to make bread, although the properties will vary somewhat, requiring some adaptation of recipes, notably to the water content. Barley and oats, although major cereal crops, are not used so much in bread making. They may, however, be added in small amounts to breads made with other flours, adding flavour, texture, and nutritional value.

Wheat gluten Gluten can be extracted from wheat and is available for use as an additive where flours are deficient in the gluten forming proteins. This is intended to help with the dough structure, improving the rise with whole grain flours. I do not use additional wheat gluten in my bread, enjoying instead the variation in density that comes with wholemeal flours.

Choice of flour(s) The choice of flour(s) for a recipe influences the texture, from light and airy to dense and heavy, and the flavour profile, from the clean taste of white wheat flour, to the nuttiness of wholemeal wheat or spelt, and rich savouriness of wholemeal rye. White wheat flour has the most capacity to develop a light bread. White bread, especially when allowed a slow fermentation, using either a preferment or sourdough culture, can have superb flavour, but it lacks the nuttiness contributed by the coarser material of a wholemeal flour. This is neither beneficial nor detrimental, but simply a matter of taste.

Adding a small amount — say, 10% — of wholemeal flour, of wheat, rye, or spelt, can contribute a degree of nutty flavour and pleasant texture but with no discernible effect on the openness of the crumb. Increasing the amount of wholemeal flour to, say, 30 to 50%, brings much of the flavour of the associated grain, whilst still allowing the white flour component to maintain a good rise, albeit with a more close, even, crumb. At levels above 50%, the bread will become increasingly dense; wholemeal wheat flour can still rise to form a loaf with good volume, spelt somewhat less so, but rye will be heavy, albeit with much flavour.

4.2.2 Water

Water is the most important variable in a bread recipe and a lack thereof is, perhaps, the single most critical defect in more than a few bread recipes. Levels of yeast and salt are readily determined from the flour weight and the method of preparation. Generally referred to as the hydration of a dough and measured as a percentage of flour weight, the ideal amount of water is rather more difficult to determine.

Water is essential for the development of gluten and for the fermentation activity of yeasts and bacteria. A wet dough will ferment more rapidly than a dry dough. It will develop better flavour and a lighter, more open crumb, potentially with a much improved oven spring — the rapid expansion of the dough during the first minutes of baking — see Section 4.8. Doughs with higher moisture necessitate different techniques if working by hand; the traditional approach to kneading will just make a mess if working with a wet, sticky, dough. Once mastered, however, these techniques are no more difficult or time consuming. In fact, whilst a wet dough is sticky it is also soft and malleable, and far less strenuous to mix and knead by hand. If working the dough by machine, a wet dough mixes better and is rather easier on the machine than a dry dough.

The challenge in specifying the most suitable hydration for a given recipe is that it depends on the prevailing conditions — notably temperature and humidity — and the properties of the flour. The protein content of the flour can have an effect, with strong flours needing more water than ordinary bread or plain flours. Wholemeal flours need more water than white flours, and rye needs a great deal more than wheat.

Thus, it is with the hydration of the dough, that the baker is first challenged to apply a measure of judgement. There is no substitute for experience, and gaining that feel for the dough under varying conditions, which will allow the baker to adapt to different flours and still produce the desired results. If the dough holds its shape well but fails to rise well, consider increasing the hydration. Conversely, if the dough fails to keep its shape, consider reducing the hydration. All of the recipes in this book assume a moderately strong bread flour. As the properties of the flour can vary, not only between brands or batches but also depending on the environment, the baker must adapt the hydration to suit. For any recipe in this book, it is a good idea to hold back a little of the water content when mixing the ingredients, then feel the dough to decide whether more water is needed. It is better to adjust the water content than the flour content as this would also necessitate adjustments to salt, yeast, and other ingredients.

Although I have baked bread for many years and experimented with various methods, it was not until I increased the hydration of my doughs that I started to get results that I was happy with. Properly hydrated dough allows for better fermentation and enzyme activity as well as having a marked effect on the texture of the bread. I have seen recipes that call for hydrations of around 55% with a strong white bread flour, which is insufficient, in my view, for reasonable bread. For this sort of flour, doughs from 55 to 60% would tend to produce a heavy loaf and 60 to 65% a bread with a lighter but still fairly even crumb. Raising this to 67 to 70%, which is the sort of hydration I would normally use, produces a fairly open, light bread. Pushing this further to 75% produces a great baguette, with fairly large, open, holes, and at 80%, the sort of very large and irregular holes typical of ciabatta. At 70%, the dough is readily worked by hand, but becomes rather more difficult if raised much further. As a starting point, 70% is not a bad choice, and many of the recipes in this book are in the high 60s to low 70s. This may be increased further as the proportion of wholemeal flour is increased; some dark rye breads may be made with a hydration of 100% or more.

4.2.3 Yeast

Bread may be made with baker's yeast — strains of yeast selected for their performance in bread making — or the wild yeasts of a sourdough culture. The latter is discussed in Chapter 8. Baker's yeast is generally available in three forms: fresh yeast, typically in compressed blocks; active dried yeast; and instant dried yeast. That most readily available to the home baker is instant dried yeast. Both instant and fresh yeast can be added directly to the flour, whereas active dried yeast needs to be rejuvenated in warm water for ten minutes or so. Fresh yeast is ideal, but has limited shelf life, which is problematic for the occasional home baker. Dried yeast, of one sort of another, has good storage properties so is rather more convenient. Thus, all of the recipes in this book that use baker's yeast are based on instant dried yeast. If using fresh yeast, multiply the quantity listed by a factor of three.

The amount of yeast used will determine, along with other factors such as hydration and temperature, how quickly preferments—portions of the flour and water that are fermented prior to making the main dough—mature, doughs ferment, and shaped loaves prove. Mass produced bread tends to include rather large amounts of yeast, by way of short-cut. Increasing the amount of yeast will result in a faster fermentation, but at the expense of flavour and structure. I prefer to use more modest amounts, allowing more time for the dough to develop, and one can go further and use just a pinch of yeast and ferment over the course of a day or two if desired. Yeast is often sold in sachets of 7 g or so, which appears to be recommended for raising around 500 g of flour. However, that amount can readily be used for 1 kg of flour, with a somewhat longer fermentation.

A good starting point is 0.3% for a preferment, and 0.75% for the dough. This quantity suits my usual schedule, with an overnight preferment, around two hours of fermentation, followed by an hour or so of final proving. One might wish to reduce the amount used in the preferment during warm weather, if prefermenting during the day rather than overnight, and if starting with warm water, as I always begin with cold water.

4.2.4 Salt

Some breads are made without the addition of salt, such as the Italian *pane Toscano*, but most include a certain amount, primarily to enhance the flavour, as unsalted bread can taste rather bland, but also with a preservative effect. A level of 1.5 to 2.25%, that is 1.5 to 2.25 g per 100 g of flour, is generally suitable. Most recipes in this book suggest 2%, but this can be adjusted according to taste. If adding salty ingredients to a dough, such as cheese, preserved products, or salted butter, consider lowering the amount of added salt. Salt has an inhibiting effect on yeast, drawing the moisture away from the yeast cells, thus it is best to mix them separately. Salt also has an interesting effect on dough, strengthening and tightening the gluten network. If added part way through kneading, which I do most often, the effect of the salt can be immediately felt in the dough. A good quality sea salt is recommended.

4.2.5 Fats and dairy

Good bread can be made with just the key ingredients of flour, water, salt, and yeast. However, fats are a common addition, present in much of the commercial bread. Fats have a tenderising effect on the crumb, shortening the strands of gluten. A less chewy and more even crumb is produced, which may or may not be desirable, depending on the sort of bread being made, and the keeping qualities of the bread are improved. In large quantities, as one might use in preparing enriched doughs such as brioche, the fat can significantly inhibit the development of the gluten. In the smaller quantities added to a normal loaf, gluten development is not unduly affected. The only fats that are added in this book are butter and olive oil, both of which contribute good flavour to the bread aside from any shortening effect they may have. I am particularly fond of using olive oil in white bread doughs. A starting point of 5 to 10% is probably appropriate.

Many recipes include milk as part or all of the liquid content. The fat content of the milk has the same effect on the crumb as any other fat. Using milk will tend to result in a softer crumb and richer flavour and, depending on the fat content, longer shelf life. The crust colour can be enhanced by the presence of the milk sugar, lactose. Fresh milk contains a substance called glutathione. This works to weaken gluten, and can result in slack loaves with poor rise. Glutathione can be deactivated by scalding — heating the milk to around 85°C — although different sources differ as to whether this is really necessary or not. Many recipes call for dried milk powder instead of fresh, being more convenient to store and not souring in warm temperatures. Nonetheless, in those recipes in which I use milk, I do prefer to use fresh organic whole milk, scalding it as a precaution. For the home baker, this is no significant inconvenience. If replacing the water in a recipe with milk, the amount of liquid may need to be increased as milk is only around 87% water, and, conversely, the amount of liquid reduced if replacing milk with water.

4.2.6 Sugars

Sugar is often included in commercial offerings, and also in many bread recipes. It is not uncommon to see a teaspoon or two added to a slurry of yeast and water, to give the yeast a feed. However, it is not, generally, necessary to add sugar, and I never add refined white sugar to my bread, as it contributes little in the way of flavour. Usually, sufficient sugar to feed the yeast is provided by the conversion of starch to sugar by amylase in the flour, and accelerating the fermentation is not beneficial to flavour. Sugar, like salt, draws moisture from the dough, and in large quantities can have an inhibiting effect on the formation of gluten, and in smaller quantities some small tenderising effect. Increasing the amount of residual sugar remaining in the dough at baking time can also contribute to crust colour. Although I do not add white sugar to any of the doughs in this book, there are breads that quite legitimately incorporate sugars in the form of, for example, honey, malt, or molasses, where they are added primarily from the perspective of flavour. As a hobby beekeeper, I have plenty of pure honey to hand, so like to have some recipes where I can use it. Except for the malt bread of Section 5.6, the use of honey, malt, or molasses, is optional.

4.2.7　Additional ingredients

Bread is often flavoured with herbs, spices, seeds, grains, nuts, cheese, fruits, and vegetables. Seeds and grains may need soaking before use, see Section 5.5, to avoid them robbing the dough of moisture and to soften them for a more pleasant eating experience. Adding such things to the dough can disrupt the gluten formation, by cutting through gluten strands. Coarse matter may therefore be better added after the dough has been developed to some degree. Herbs and spices do not generally pose any problems and can be added to the dough at any stage. Ingredients such as nuts or olives would interfere with the development of the dough and also be damaged by the kneading process, so are best added at the end of kneading or prior to shaping. Some ingredients, notably vegetables, bring added moisture, and are ideally salted and/or cooked so as to remove excess liquid. It is best to be a little cautious when incorporating extra ingredients into a recipe, as they can interfere with the rise and produce a stodgy bread, particularly where moisture is absorbed or released.

4.3　Mixing of ingredients

The objective of mixing is to produce a fairly homogeneous mass from the flour, water, and other ingredients. Gluten development is another matter, and treated below. Mixing should be performed at a low speed, if using a mixer; for wet doughs, this may be done with the beater attachment or the dough hook. Refer to the manufacturer's instructions for the appropriate speed setting. It is at the mixing stage that the baker must first use a measure of judgement, in ensuring the correct hydration of the dough, so that it has the desired properties through the rest of the process. This is something that can only come through experience. Flour varies depending on the properties of the grain and the humidity, and so one may need to hold back a little water or add extra based on the feel of the dough. So, with every recipe in this book, even though they have been tested under my kitchen conditions, it is wise to hold back a little of the water content of the main dough — not for any preferments that might be included, see Chapter 7 — and check the consistency of the dough before adding the rest, or even a little extra if deemed necessary. For most recipes, the dough should feel a bit wet and sticky, unleavened breads being one exception. A stiff dry dough is not intended with any of the yeasted breads. Until one is comfortable handling such doughs, there may be the temptation to reduce the water content or add more flour to make a more stiff and less sticky dough, but this is best resisted as the bread will suffer.

It takes time for the water to fully hydrate the flour. Thus, it is somewhat premature to move directly to developing the gluten, through mechanical or hand kneading. In a method promoted by Professor Raymond Calvel, known as *autolyse* — from autolysis — a rest period is included between mixing and kneading. This can be anything from 15 minutes to an hour or so. This time allows the flour to fully absorb the water and for the various enzymes to begin to work on the flour. In this approach, the yeast and salt are held back until the autolyse is complete, salt interfering with enzyme activity and the proper hydration of the flour. Hence, this is also known as the delayed salt method. Where preferments or sourdough cultures are used, these may also need to be included at the start, as there may otherwise be insufficient water in the dough to properly hydrate the flour.

The benefits of an autolyse become clear when one begins to knead the dough, which takes markedly less time. Beyond the reduction in effort, one may find improved structure and flavour, especially where a reduction in mechanical kneading is realised — see below. Wherever it makes sense to do so, my recipes do include this rest period between initial mixing and kneading. For the home baker, it makes a lot of sense, especially where kneading by hand.

4.4 Development of gluten

The usual approach to the development of the gluten in the dough is largely a mechanical one, conducted either using a mixer, or by hand methods. This kneading, which involves repeated stretching of the dough to encourage the gluten forming proteins to link, is, in some ways, a short cut to gluten formation. Gluten will develop without such mechanical input. After an hour of autolyse, described above, one can already observe the formation of some gluten. In a mature preferment or sourdough culture, which has had nothing more than a quick stir to combine the flour and the water, it will be quite evident that the process of fermentation develops a great deal of gluten without outside assistance. With a lengthy fermentation one can create bread without any kneading, and there are many advocates of so called no-knead bread. In my experience, the no-knead approach can make good bread, but does not produce the best bread. For example, the 'ten minute bread' described in Section 1.1 is remarkably good for almost no effort, but it falls rather short of the baguette of Section 7.2.

Excessive high speed mechanical kneading that commercial dough may experience is an important reason for poor quality bread. High speed mixing causes the oxidisation of the dough, destroying the carotenoids, pigments that are responsible for the creamy colour of artisan bread as well as much flavour. Even bread made with white flour should not be that white, and if it is, then it has been much damaged by the manufacturing process. It is possible to overwork a dough if kneading by machine, although most unlikely if working by hand. Overworked dough will be too tight to have any extensibility, and the tight gluten network may break down; in either event, the texture will suffer.

Although excessive kneading can be harmful, and some bread recipes require little or no kneading, in general one would expect to work the dough to a certain degree to develop the gluten. The trick is to do so more gently and only just as much as is needed. Ultimately, one is trying to provide enough strength in the dough to hold its shape and capture the carbon dioxide produced during fermentation, but with the right balance of elasticity and extensibility so that it can be shaped without tearing, and rise well in proving and baking. This is another area in which experience must be acquired; if the dough lacks strength when shaped or the bake is poor, then more time may need to be spent developing the gluten.

Mixed dough, even with an autolyse step, will be a shaggy mess, with little structure. With the sort of hydration levels used in most of the recipes in this book, it will be quite sticky. As the dough is worked, though, it will transform into a much less sticky, smooth dough, that is nicely elastic. The dough when first stretched, will tear and shred, then, as the gluten is developed, it will stretch

The window pane test—the dough is sufficiently elastic to stretch without tearing until almost transparent

without tearing. One commonly mentioned test of gluten development is referred to as the window pane test. A portion of dough is stretched out gently until it is almost thin enough to see through, showing that the gluten is properly developed.

The initial kneading of the dough is not the only way to develop strength. The method known commonly as *stretch and fold* can be used during fermentation to quite effectively build the strength of the dough. This is a simple matter of stretching the dough and folding it over several times, either on the bench, or in the bowl or container in which it is fermenting. A fold during the fermentation process is often a good idea, as the gluten can relax during this period. It might seem that a simple fold would have little affect, but its impact on dough strength is often quite remarkable. It is always a matter of balance, though, and too many folds can build too much strength, making shaping more difficult.

Besides kneading and folding, there are numerous factors that effect the development of gluten in the dough. The first is the composition of the flour. Flours high in the gluten forming proteins can obviously develop a stronger dough, but the higher the amount of protein, the more work is needed to fully develop the gluten. Wholemeal flours and those with coarse particles have the effect of cutting the gluten strands, so a mixture of, say, half white and half wholemeal flour cannot be expected to develop quite as well as a dough made entirely with white flour. Doughs with substantial amounts of rye need less kneading as there will be little gluten development and the structure of the rye is readily damaged through over working, to the point where a 100% rye bread is not kneaded at all. The use of a preferment or sourdough culture — see Chapters 7 and 8 — reduces the amount of kneading required, as these bring a certain amount of gluten development and the acids occurring during fermentation, see below, lend strength to the dough.

The commercial baker may be forced to develop the dough using a mixer. The home baker has a choice of using a mixer or hand methods. A mixer can be useful for working with particularly wet doughs, but there is no substitute for hand methods. I will often use the mixer for rustling up a quick focaccia or pizza dough, but generally prefer to prepare my dough by hand. In either case, the home baker is well advised to prepare doughs first by hand, until familiarity with the feel of the dough is acquired. One can reduce the harm caused by mechanical kneading by reducing the kneading time and then working the dough a little by hand, or incorporating a number of folds into the fermentation period. Still, the home baker is not likely to be causing nearly so much damage to the dough as the large scale commercial baker, even if using a mixer for the entire process. Kneading is generally carried out at a higher speed than mixing, and for this purpose a dough hook is probably best. Refer to the manufacturer's instructions for the appropriate speed setting.

Although one could adopt a simple process, mixing all of the ingredients and immediately kneading the dough until the gluten is fully developed, I favour a slower approach that is arguably better for the bread and, although taking more time, takes less effort on the part of the baker. My general approach is to: mix dry and wet ingredients, excluding yeast and salt; autolyse for one hour; mix in the yeast; knead for a few minutes, until the dough is smooth; cover and rest for ten minutes; add the salt and knead for another few minutes; ferment for two hours or so, folding the dough several times.

The rest in between the first and second kneading session is not entirely conventional, but something I started doing when I began delaying the addition of the salt, and it works well for me. Feel free to experiment with the process and find something that works well, and consistently so. As soon as the salt is added, the dough tightens up, and it does not take too long before the dough is completely smooth and elastic. In this slow process, the kneading sessions only need to be a few minutes each. Many of the breads I make on a regular basis include a preferment or sourdough culture. The strength that this brings to the dough is readily observed, and these doughs come together even more quickly.

Working by hand, the method of kneading will, of necessity, vary according to the hydration of the dough. The sort of kneading that one often sees, of a fairly stiff dough, on a well floured worktop, is not appropriate for the levels of hydration in most of the recipes in this book. Methods of working the dough, under different conditions, are described in Section 4.9.

4.5 Bulk fermentation

Bulk fermentation is, perhaps, oddly named for the home baker. When baking a large batch of bread, the mixing, kneading, and initial fermentation of the dough, are done in bulk, then the dough is divided for shaping. For the home baker, the dough might only be destined for one or two loaves.

All manner of complex processes are going on during the fermentation, the important by-products of which are strength, flavour, and the capture of fermentation gases. Yeast feeds on sugars in the flour, producing carbon dioxide in the process. There is a limited amount of free sugar in the flour, but enzymes, notably amylase, work to convert starch to sugar that the yeast can consume. The formation of bubbles of carbon dioxide, trapped within the dough, causes it to rise, doubling or even tripling in size. Yeast is not the only active party in fermentation. Bacteria are also at work, especially in sourdough, producing acids, most notably lactic acid, but also acetic acid. These develop the flavour but also increase the strength of the dough.

Whilst yeasts can develop a dough rather quickly at their optimal temperatures, the work of bacteria is slower, so bread produced quickly will be lacking in the acidic compounds. It is for this reason that preferments are used. Discussed further in Chapter 7, preferments are, as the name suggests, portions of dough — generally only flour, water, and a little yeast — that are allowed to ferment for an extended period, such as overnight. A preferment has the time for the bacteria to work and for gluten to develop naturally. Added to the main dough, these bring immediate benefits of strength and flavour. A short fermentation cannot develop the flavour potential of the dough, and, despite the efforts of the large commercial bakeries, there are no shortcuts to true bread flavour. As the acidity of the dough increases, the keeping qualities improve. Bread baked from a slow fermentation or using a sourdough culture will keep better than the equivalent straight dough.

Although long and slow fermentations develop much flavour, there is a limit to how long one may do so before the structure of the dough is weakened. Although mechanical input, from fermentation, or from folding, and the acidification of the dough, contribute to increasing strength, other factors are at work, such as the enzyme protease, that weaken the gluten. This can be beneficial to extensibility, that is, allowing one to more easily shape the dough, especially useful if shaping baguettes or similar long forms, or for pizza dough which must be stretched thinly. However, this weakening can go too far, and can be problematic if one is retarding a batch of dough, either during bulk fermentation or final prove, by placing in the refrigerator or other cool location. This might be desirable, for example, to enable one to prepare a batch of dough one day and bake it the next, but it brings extra challenges.

A number of factors will affect the rate of fermentation, including: the amount of yeast used; the presence of sugars and level of amylase; the amount of salt; and the amount of water, wet dough fermenting more quickly and effectively than dry dough. Temperature, though, is the most significant factor in the activity of the yeast, and also in the activity of amylase. The most suitable temperature for proving bread is generally considered to be somewhere around 25°C, so rather warmer than normal room temperature. Although the production of carbon dioxide will increase with higher temperatures, fermenting at a faster rate is detrimental to the flavour and strength of the dough. Activity will start to decline above 40°C, and temperatures somewhere above 50°C will kill the yeast cells. Dropping much below 20°C will slow development, although the yeast will still be active even if placed in the refrigerator, only at a much reduced rate. Amylase works better at higher temperatures than one would normally hold the dough, being particularly active around 50°C, which is too high for the yeast.

The commercial baker may take steps to bring the dough to the desired fermentation temperature by calculating the correct water temperature needed to raise the temperature of the entire dough, and then maintaining the environment, using a proving cabinet, to provide controlled temperature and humidity so that the process is as repeatable as possible. This careful control of the temperature may be necessary in the commercial environment, where a lack of repeatability might impact on production, but the home baker has rather less to worry about. One can generally bake as and when the dough is ready, fermenting at whatever the room temperature happens to be, and accepting that it may take a little more or less time than usual depending on the conditions. Fermentation may also be retarded by refrigeration, during the bulk fermentation stage or the final prove, to hold back a batch of dough. I often do this myself with flatbread recipes, which will develop slowly in the refrigerator for several days.

Many bread recipes for the home baker will specify warm water, perhaps hand hot, or one third boiling and two thirds cold tap water, for the mix. One area in which I generally depart from the more commonly accepted approach is that I start with cold water, most often filtered water straight from the fridge. No doubt this slows the fermentation process somewhat, but I generally feel this is not a bad thing. Whilst one is often encouraged to place the fermenting dough in a warm location, I prefer a cooler spot where the dough will develop a little more slowly.

4.6 Dividing and shaping

This stage of the bread process turns the batch of dough into individual loaves. The weight of ingredients in the dough should have been calculated with the number and final weights of the individual loaves in mind — refer to Section 1.4.2. The dough is gently tipped out of the bowl or other container in which it is has been fermenting and, with the aid of scales as needed, divided into suitable portions according to the form of bread being prepared. For those baked in tins, I prefer a 2 lb loaf tin, requiring 900 g to 1 kg of dough. Boules and batards can be anywhere from 500 g to 1.5 kg. Batons that can fit in a domestic oven can be scaled at 200 to 250 g, whilst baguettes, for those that have the means to bake them, may be 300 to 400 g. Rolls can be anywhere from 50 g to 100 g, with 70 g being a good starting point.

Dividing the dough — the green plate is sitting on a set of digital scales; small pieces of dough are cut as needed to make up the desired weight

Once portioned up, the individual pieces of dough are then degassed — gently patted down to remove the large and inconsistent bubbles of gas — and shaped accordingly. It is at this point that some recipes refer to *punching down* the dough or *knocking back*, and one can see this being done with more vigour than is warranted; all it needs is a gentle pat. One can occasionally see the dough given a quick knead before shaping, and this, in my view, is unnecessary and detrimental.

Shaping is not just about forming an appropriate shape — round for boules and rolls, elongated for batards or for placing in loaf tins, long and thin for baguettes, and so on — it is about getting strength into the dough so that it will hold its shape. That strength comes from surface tension, stretching the outside of the dough, without tearing, so that it is taut. It is at this point that one may discover that the dough is weak, in that it is easily shaped but lacks the tension needed to hold that shape, or that it is too strong to be easily shaped — most often a problem when shaping baguettes, focaccia, fougasse, pizza, or other form where the dough must be stretched considerably.

If the dough is a bit too tight, it can be shaped loosely, then left to rest on the bench before final shaping. In fact, this step of *preshaping* is commonly discussed in bread books and likely to be carried out when working on a larger scale, but less significant at home. The home baker may or may not need to rest the dough at this stage. The notion with preshaping is to allow any excessive tightness from working the dough to relax to allow the final shaping to be done without damaging the dough. It is most important that the dough is not torn during shaping. Preshaping takes each piece of dough and gently forms it, typically into a round shape, then rests it before final shaping, when the surface tension is really built up. The rest period may vary from a few minutes to twenty minutes or more depending on the tightness of the dough and the shape to be formed.

4.7   Final prove

The final prove of the dough is that stage where shaped loaves are allowed to rise in volume before they are scored and baked. Different breads are proved in different ways. Some, especially baguettes and similar shapes, may be placed on well floured cloths, seams of which are pulled up to keep the individual loaves separate. Typically of raw linen, such a cloth is known as a *couche*. Couche material may be bought by the metre, but linen tea towels of a thick grade may also be suitable for the home baker. Another towel, or length of couche cloth can then be used to cover the loaves as they prove. If one has the equipment, the loaves may be transferred from the couche to a peel using a flipping board, also known as a *planchette a pain*. The use of couche in this manner is particularly useful when making a large batch of baguettes or similar. Other breads may be proved on baking sheets ready to be transferred directly to the oven or to be moved to a baking stone. Some recommend proving on baking parchment, which has the advantage that it is easily transferred to the oven; I do not generally use this method myself, but can imagine where it may be helpful. For the traditional sliced loaf, the shaped dough is placed in tins to prove and, subsequently, bake. Finally, and most important for sourdoughs that have a long final prove and other doughs that need a little help to hold their shape, bread may be proved in a banneton, also known as a brotform or proving basket. Typically of cane, which is well floured before placing in the shaped dough, a banneton gives the bread not only a good shape but also a decorative finish, leaving impressions of the canes on the surface of the baked bread.

Batons and rolls proving on couche and then transferred to a peel for scoring and loading

Timing the final prove is another matter of judgement that must be acquired through practice. It will vary between different sorts of bread. A strong white dough may readily double in size before it is ready, whereas a sourdough may be ready when it has increased by only half as much. If in doubt, err on the side of under proving the dough. If substantially under proved, the baked loaf will be a little on the dense side, but an over proved loaf may collapse, as the gluten becomes stretched beyond its ability to sustain the structure of the loaf. One may test the condition of the dough by gently probing with a finger, depressing the dough. If the dough springs back immediately, it is an indication of plenty of pressure inside the dough, and it may be left to prove a while longer. If the dough springs back over the course of a few seconds, perhaps leaving a small imprint, the dough is likely to be ready to bake. If the impression remains, there is insufficient pressure in the dough, and it be over proved. It should be baked immediately, but may suffer either a poor increase in volume in the oven — see below — or collapse.

As with bulk fermentation, temperature is the most significant variable in the time for the final prove. At normal room temperatures, doughs prepared with baker's yeast will take around 60 to 90 minutes, whilst sourdough will take rather longer, perhaps five to eight hours. It is possible to retard shaped loaves by refrigeration or placing in an otherwise cool location, but one must contend with the ongoing weakening of the dough, and ensure that the dough has sufficient strength in the first place so that it will perform well when finally baked. Shaped dough can be placed in a suitable container, so that it can be covered but allowed room to develop, and refrigerated. If timed right, it can be removed from the refrigerator when the oven is switched on to heat and be ready to bake once the oven, and any baking stone or other vessel, has reached temperature, after about one hour. If the loaves have not developed sufficiently, allow some extra time at room temperature. Some experimentation may well be needed to get the schedule right, but for fresh baked loaves in the morning, this option may be rather more attractive for the home baker than working through the night. Some breads, such as the flatbreads of Chapter 6, respond well to retardation, indeed benefitting in flavour, texture, and, especially, ease of shaping, where the dough becomes much more extensible after a couple of days in the refrigerator. After a long, slow, ferment, these need little time to prove, and can be shaped whilst the oven heats.

4.8   Scoring and baking

As soon as a loaf is placed in a hot oven, there is a rapid, albeit brief, surge of activity, causing, hopefully, a marked inflation of the dough; a phenomenon known as oven spring or bounce. Scoring is often important in enabling this rise. Without scoring, the tension of the outside of the bread will tend to resist the rise and, as the crust begins to form, the bread will not be able to expand. An unscored, or poorly scored, loaf will often rupture in an *ad hoc* way. To allow expansion and control the appearance of the finished loaf, it can be scored, usually with a razor blade—often mounted on a handle known as a lame—or a sharp knife. The loaf will then expand in a controlled way, and these fine cuts will open decoratively during the bake.

Scoring can be done in different ways and in various patterns. If the blade is held perpendicular to the surface of the loaf, and scored deeply, say, 1 cm or so in depth, the cut will tend to open without tearing. If held at the shallow angle, say, 30 to 40°, and scored more gently, perhaps around ½ cm in depth, the loaf will tend to tear as the cuts open up, and a lip, known as an *ear*, will form on one side of the cut, lending a rustic appearance that is common amongst well made artisan bread.

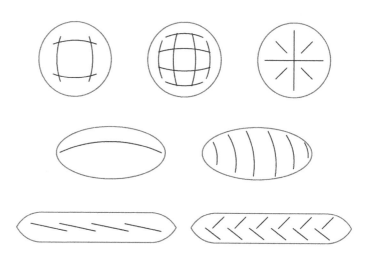

Assortment of suitable scoring patterns for boules (top), batards (centre), and batons (bottom)

The extent to which a loaf opens up will depend on several factors, including: the way it is scored; the effective use of steam during the early part of the bake—see below; and the condition of the loaf after final prove—the cuts will open more dramatically if baked whilst there is still good pressure within the loaf, and much less so as it begins to over prove.

Some rolls, shaped like small batards or batons, can be scored as for the larger sorts, but the common round roll is not usually scored. There is, then, the danger that the rolls will burst, due to insufficient expansion of the crust. To reduce or avoid this, in addition to covering during proving, one can spray the surface with water before baking. I usually cover bread with a linen tea towel whilst proving. For rolls, covering

Rustic tear and characteristic ear on a classic batard

with a damp tea towel might better help prevent the surface from drying out.

A commercial bread oven, such as might be used by an artisan baker, has two features that are absent from a typical home oven: a stone floor, and steam injection. The heat in the floor provides a perfect base on which to bake bread, ensuring that the bottom of the loaf is properly cooked. Steam is also important, and is injected during the first few minutes of the bake, where it prevents the crust of the bread from setting up too quickly. Without steam, the crust will form prematurely, and will curtail any further rise, thus without steam one cannot achieve maximum loaf volume. After some minutes, the crust will begin to form and the steam is no longer helpful, so is vented to allow the desired crisp golden crust to develop. Such an oven provides an environment not unlike that of the traditional wood fired oven.

Aside from building a wood fired oven, there are ways of providing a better environment for home made bread. First, one can use a baking stone. Typically made of clay fired to a high temperature, this is placed on an oven shelf and allowed to heat for some time before baking. It facilitates improved transference of heat to the base of the bread, helping with oven spring and good baking of the bottom of the loaf. In my view, a baking stone is an almost essential investment that will much improve the baking of various breads and enable good pizza to be made at home, despite not being able to reach the high temperatures of a proper pizza oven. Second, one can provide steam, either by misting the oven with a sprayer or by throwing water in a hot pan or tray near the bottom of the oven. I adopt the latter and am generally satisfied with the results, although I suspect that it is not nearly so effective as with a purpose built bread oven. After five to ten minutes, the oven door can be opened to allow any excess steam to escape.

A covered vessel of either cast iron — a Dutch oven — or clay can be used to bake bread. This is heated in the oven much like a baking stone. Used mainly for round shaped loaves —

boules — the hot vessel is removed from the oven, the lid taken off, the base dusted with flour, the bread tipped in from its proving basket, scored if desired, the lid put back on, and then returned to the oven. The lid is removed for the latter portion of the bake. Moisture from the bread is retained within the vessel, providing the steam needed for a good rise. Such a vessel is somewhat limited in scope, but a boule is one of the more common forms for artisan bread, so one might wish to try this approach. A cast iron casserole dish with a lid can serve quite well, although there are products, such as the well known *La Cloche* 'baking dome', that are designed for this specific purpose; see, for example, the photograph of the spelt bread of Section 5.4.

Optimal baking times and temperatures vary according not only to the size of the loaf but also the desired characteristics of the finished bread. Both the internal and external temperatures are significant. Certain recipes are more inclined to develop a robust crust, such as the semolina bread of Section 7.5, or the baguette of Section 7.2, whilst others, particularly those incorporating fats and dairy, such as the milk bread of Section 5.3, are more likely to have a soft crust. Crusty breads are typically baked at a higher temperature than those intended to have a soft crust.

The baking temperatures used in this book range from 190 to 250°C, with the exception of certain flatbreads, for which the maximum setting — 275°C for my ovens — is used. These temperatures are for a conventional setting, with top and bottom heat; I do not use the fan setting, but if there is no choice, reduce the temperatures in accordance with the manufacturer's instructions; perhaps 10 to 20°C. I generally bake on the middle or lower-middle shelf, depending on the height of the loaf. For most breads, I begin the bake at 250°C and reduce to 220°C part way through. For a soft roll, which does not want a hard crust, or a loaf tin, where the top can darken considerably before the rest of the loaf is properly cooked, I bake at a lower temperature of 190 to 220°C. As a loaf tin protects the sides of the bread and reduces colourisation, I often remove the loaf from the tin five or ten minutes before the end of cooking and put it back in the oven to develop a more even colour.

The traditional way of telling whether a loaf is done is by look and feel, and with a tap on the base, which should have a distinctive hollow sound. It is particularly challenging to achieve a crusty loaf that retains that crust after cooling as residual moisture inside the loaf softens the crust, and that is where the internal temperature of the bread becomes especially important. A commonly quoted figure is 190°F, which equates to approximately 88°C, but, personally, I think this is too low for most loaves. Temperatures around 90°C might be suitable for a soft bread, but something around 95°C is probably more generally suitable. For a good crusty hearth bread, I like to get the internal temperature up to 98 to 99°C — 208 to 212°F — rather more than is often recommended. The result, though, is a good crust that generally remains fairly crisp after cooling. Note that environmental conditions can also be problematic, excessive humidity rapidly softening the crust. Unless baking a sequence of loaves, one can switch off the oven, leaving the bread where it is, open the door a little, and leave in the residual heat for some minutes to help further dry the bread out. It is better to err on the side of over baked, rather than under baked, as the latter may be doughy and unpalatable. For establishing a suitable baking schedule for a new recipe, a digital instant read temperature probe is a useful tool, allowing the internal temperature to be quickly and accurately measured. Even after baking the same recipe several times, I still find it useful to double check the temperatures.

The schedule that I usually adopt for baking is to heat the oven to an initial temperature, up to an hour in advance, so that the baking stone that I use for most breads is properly heated through. I also place a heavy pan near the bottom of the oven for generating steam. I add the loaves along with a cup of hot water to the tray to generate the steam. After ten minutes, I open the oven door to allow any excess steam to escape, lower the temperature to its final setting, and allow the oven to cool a little before closing the door. The following table provides an approximate guide to baking temperatures and times, which are broadly applicable throughout the book. For a more crusty result, consider extending the first period by five minutes and reduce the overall bake accordingly. One might wish to experiment with higher and lower temperatures and different schedules, but these temperatures should serve as a reasonable starting point. Ovens vary considerably, so any timings suggested in this book can only be approximate guidelines. For larger loaves, a longer bake at the lower temperature will be needed.

bread form	typical weight (g)	T initial (°C)	T final (°C)	total time (mins)
baton	300	250	220	20–25
boule or batard	500	250	220	30–40
boule or batard	1000	250	220	35–45
crusty roll	80	250	220	18–22
soft roll	80	200	200	20–25
2 lb loaf tin	950	220	200	40–55

The final part of the bake happens when the bread is removed from the oven, and continues until the bread is cool. It should be placed on a wire rack and allowed good airflow to maintain the crust. Unlike unleavened breads and those leavened with baking soda, yeasted breads are best allowed to cool completely before slicing. If sliced whilst still warm, the loaf may tear, and residual moisture in the crumb will lend it a doughy texture. If warm bread is desired, it is arguably better to allow the bread to cool completely, then reheat when needed for a few minutes in a moderate oven, rather than eating before it is ready. A few minutes in the oven can also help to restore a softened crust.

4.9 Working with the dough

Two areas of the bread making craft in particular require some practice; one is in the kneading of the dough, and the other in shaping. There are various ways in which dough can be worked; this section illustrates a few of those that I find most useful.

4.9.1 Mixing, kneading, and folding

Mixing is a simple matter of combining the ingredients to form a uniform mass. This may be done using a stand mixer on low speed, or in a mixing bowl or tub of some sort. Although one could use a wooden spoon, spatula, or dough whisk, the dough scraper is most often the ideal tool for the job. Mixing in a bowl, a folding action, combined with rotation of the bowl, will quickly bring the ingredients together.

There are many ways of kneading the dough, and in some ways it is not particularly important how it is worked, so long as the dough is stretched and folded to develop the gluten. The method one chooses will, of necessity, vary depending on the hydration of the dough. The traditional method is to knead the dough on a floured surface, stretching the dough out with the heel of the hand and then rolling or folding the dough back. This works well enough for doughs with relatively low amounts of water, but will work poorly with most of the recipes in this book. Doughs with a reasonable amount of water will be too sticky; they will pick up so much flour that the properties of the dough will be altered. Some recommend working the dough on an oiled surface, but I am not fond of this solution, as I do not like the way the dough comes together when the surface gets oily. The oil is absorbed into the dough, affecting the flavour, texture, and the crust, which may be fine for some recipes, but not desirable for others.

As it happens, it is not nearly as difficult as one might imagine to knead even a wet dough on an unfloured and unoiled surface. One cannot do this by stretching out with the heel of the hand, of course, without getting into a mess, but using finger tips only, and with the aid of the dough scraper as and when needed, the dough can be stretched and folded with ease. As the dough comes together, it is the very stickiness that helps with this method. The fascinating thing when hand working a wet dough is feeling how it changes as it develops, losing much of its stickiness during the process. I do not use any flour or oil when kneading any of the yeasted doughs in this book. The only dough that might cause problems in this regard is the ciabatta of Section 7.6, which, at 80% hydration, would be a bit tricky to work with. For that recipe, I generally just fold the dough in the bowl, and rely more on the slow fermentation to develop the dough. The baguette of Section 7.2, at 75%, is still quite readily worked by hand. Those doughs prepared with a preferment are easier to work, as they come together more quickly.

For most recipes, I use one of two similar methods, depending on the amount of dough. The first, which may be known as the *slap and fold* method or be referred to as *French kneading*, uses both hands to slap and stretch the dough, and works best with reasonable amounts of dough, say, in the order of 2 to 3 kg. The dough is first tipped out onto the worktop, and formed up using the dough scraper. Using finger tips and thumbs only, it is scooped up from the rear, lifted away from the worktop, then slapped back down. Keeping a grip on the dough, it is stretched then folded over. The dough should not be allowed to settle on the worktop for more than a moment, as it will stick, but should be picked up immediately, this time from the side, so that it is rotated at each fold. At first the dough will tear, but as it comes together, try to avoid tearing when stretching. The sequence of movements — scooping up the dough, slapping it down, stretching, and folding — will

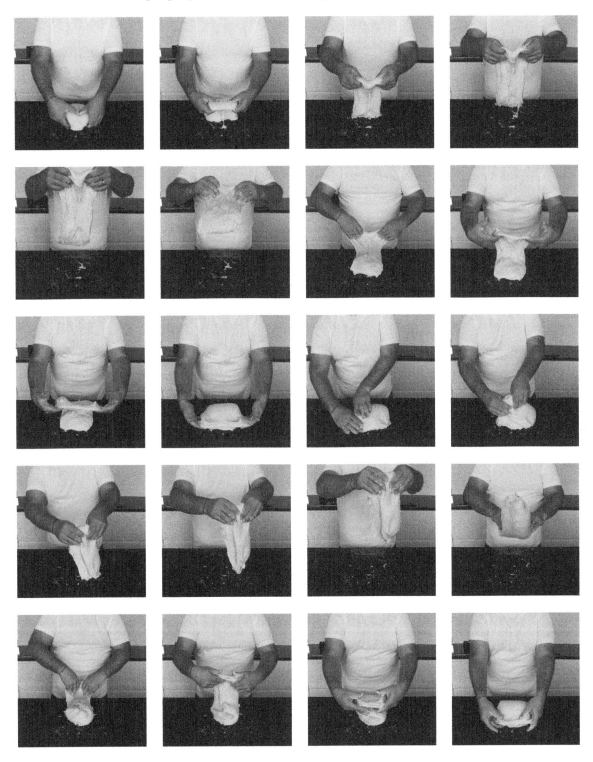

Kneading a wet dough, slapping and folding with both hands

become second nature with a little practice. As and when necessary, pause to scrape up any stuck bits of dough from the worktop. The outside of the dough quickly becomes much less sticky than the inside, so avoid rough handling, trying not to penetrate the dough when scooping it up.

For smaller amounts of dough, I find it more convenient and faster to slap and stretch the dough with one hand, using the other just to help fold the dough over. As I am right handed, I use my right hand to grab the right hand side of the dough, lift it from the worktop, and slap it down. As I stretch it, the left hand gently pinches it in the middle, between thumb and a couple of fingers, and, with a flick of the wrist, flips it over.

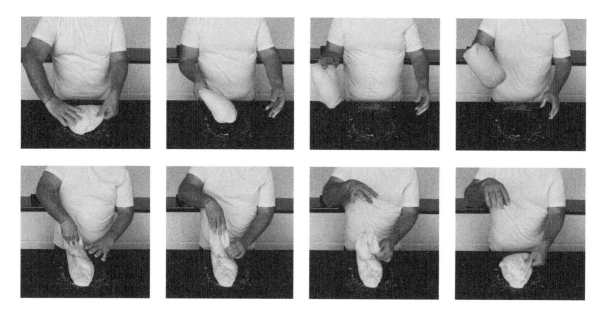

Kneading a wet dough, slapping with one hand and folding with the other

In both cases, it is the very fact that the dough will tend to stick to the worktop that allows it to be so easily worked. Without that stickiness, the dough cannot be so readily stretched, which may become apparent towards the end of kneading. With especially wet doughs, such as used for ciabatta or baguettes with high hydration, this method may prove awkward. The dough scraper can be used, though, to help stretch and fold the dough. With wet dough, a wet scraper and wet hands are more effective than using flour to prevent too much sticking.

For those few doughs that I prepare with low hydrations, notably those for unleavened bread, I will knead with the heel of the hand in the conventional way. For small amounts, this can be done one handed. Starting with a ball of dough, the heel of the hand presses down and moves away from the body to stretch out the dough. The fingers grasp the end of the dough and, in one smooth movement, fold or roll the dough back into a ball. If preferred, the dough can be worked first with the right hand, then the left, stretching the dough out diagonally on the worktop first one way then the other. One can work the dough quickly this way without straining one arm more than the other. For larger amounts of dough, work it with both hands, anchoring with one hand whilst stretching out with the heel of the other, then folding or rolling back and repeating. I usually manage to knead this way without adding flour to the worktop, but a thin dusting can be used if absolutely necessary. Avoid, though, folding dry flour into the dough, as this may not hydrate properly and any seams so formed may be evident in the finished bread.

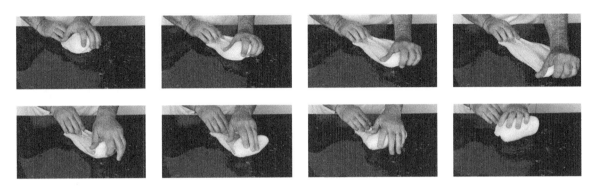

Kneading a dry dough, anchoring with one hand and stretching and rolling the dough with the other

Many doughs can benefit from folds during bulk fermentation, which help considerably to build strength, and reduce the kneading required, which is certainly to the benefit of the baker and arguably also better for the bread. Some recipes avoid a conventional kneading stage entirely, relying on folding and fermentation alone to develop the dough. Dough can be folded in the bowl or container in which it is fermenting, or can be tipped out onto the worktop. For most doughs, one can lightly dust the worktop with flour, tip out the dough, being careful not to tear it, then stretch and fold in both directions before returning to continue fermentation. As the folds are made, excess flour should be brushed off carefully, so as not to incorporate seams of dry flour into the dough. The operation takes only moments with a little practice. If necessary, use the dough scraper to assist in folding, and for the wettest doughs, forego the dusting of flour and have a bowl of water handy to keep hands and scraper wet. Under these conditions I prefer to fold in the bowl or container, with wet hands or a little olive oil to prevent excess sticking; see the ciabatta recipe, Section 7.6, for an example. Only where the recipe already includes olive oil would I consider using oil, in the bowl or container, or on the worktop, to assist with the folding. Most of the doughs in this book, although starting out quite sticky, are not at all problematic by the time the first fold is called for.

4.9.2 Shaping

There are as many forms to bread as the imagination can create. Shaping is the art of turning dough into these forms, but it is more than merely bringing the dough into shape.

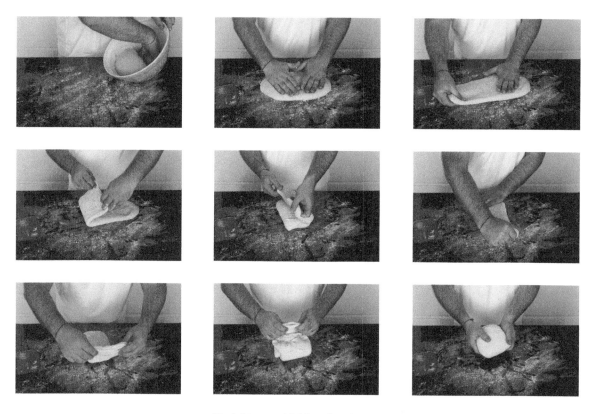

Stretching and folding the dough

It is necessary to work the dough in such a way that it has the strength to hold the form. Shaping involves folding and stretching the dough so that the outside becomes taut, and it is this tension on the surface of the dough that gives the form strength. It is important not to tear the dough, so if it lacks the extensibility needed to shape, allow it to rest on the worktop, for anywhere from a few minutes to half an hour according to the condition of the dough. The most useful forms are: a round form, known as a boule, which is common to the artisan loaf, and, on a smaller scale, rolls; a long cylindrical shape, from which are prepared such forms as the baguette, baton, and ficelle; and a tapered elongated form, known as a batard, that sits somewhere between the two, and is common for a rustic loaf. The same techniques can be applied to produce large loaves and small rolls, although for the latter one might use only one hand during tensioning. Shaping these main forms is not hard, although it takes some practice to get it right.

Shaping develops a taut outer surface whilst underneath will be a seam where the dough has been folded and pinched together. It is important to keep track of where this seam is when shaping, as one will eventually bake the bread with seam down. The final proving of the dough may be with seam up or seam down, according to what is being made and how. If proving in a banneton, the seam is kept up. Rolls, boules, and most shapes where one might prove, and perhaps even bake, on a baking sheet, are placed seam side down. Some forms, such as baguettes can be proved either way, but when baked, the seam is always on the bottom.

Unlike kneading, where I rarely use any flour, shaping needs, generally, a light dusting of flour on the worktop as the dough might be torn or otherwise mistreated if allowed to stick to the surface. One must be careful, though, not to incorporate much flour into the dough as it is shaped, else seams of dry flour may be evident in the finished bread or the seam itself fail to seal properly.

There are various ways in which the main bread forms may be shaped. Here I have described and illustrated an approach that should be easy to replicate. Once mastered, it is worth exploring other methods of shaping; as one becomes experienced with handling dough, somewhat faster methods may be considered. To form a boule, take the portion of dough and gently degas with a few pats. Pick a starting point around the rim, pinch the dough at that point, stretch it a little, then fold into the middle. Work around the rim, folding the

Shaping a boule

53

dough into the middle. Continue to stretch the dough in this way until a reasonable ball is formed, pinching the seam together if it does not stick properly. Turn the dough over, and, with cupped hands, tighten the outside of the ball until it feels taut. To achieve this, the force is applied to the base with the little fingers and edge of the palm, tucking gently under the boule and drawing the dough forward. This action will cause the front edge to stick a little and pull the outside of the dough tight. There must be a certain amount of friction between dough and worktop to tighten in this way. Too much flour will interfere with this process. Rotate the boule and repeat to tighten in all directions as needed.

Shaping a baton

To form a baton, or similar, take a portion of dough, gently degas with a few pats, stretching it out a little so that it is elongated. With this form, the idea is to fold along the length, making a tight seam. First, fold the dough from the furthest side into the middle of the dough, pressing with fingertips or the heel of the hand along the seam to seal. Turn it around and do the same from the other side. Fold the dough a final time, bringing the far edge over to the front edge, sealing the seam by pressing along its length with the base of the palm. Now there should be a tight cylinder that can be rolled gently, with cupped hands, into whatever length is needed.

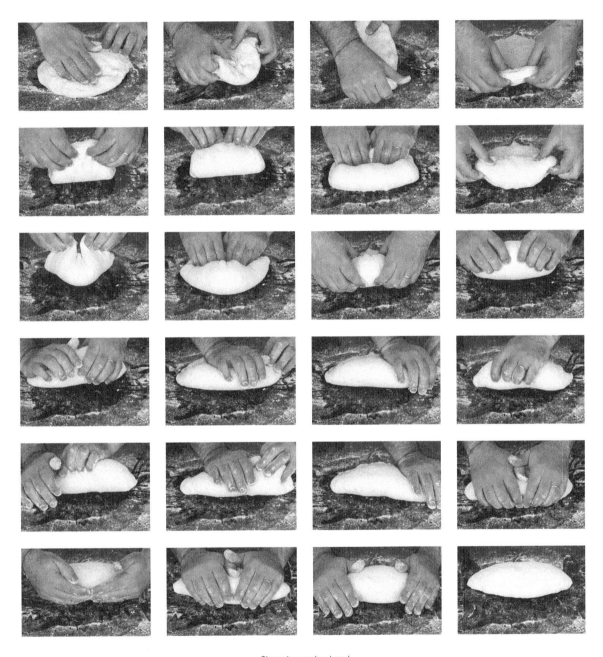

Shaping a batard

Forming a batard is similar to forming a baton, except that, having made the first fold, the corners are folded in towards the centre. This develops the somewhat humped middle and tapered end shapes that are characteristic of the form. The dough is rolled forward half way to the front edge, sealed with the base of the hand, then rolled over to line up with the front edge and sealed for the final time. The ends can be left blunt, tucked in during the folds, or rolled to a point, according to preference. The batard may be elongated as needed by rolling, much as for a baton.

5. Basic yeast breads

In this chapter are recipes for so-called straight or direct doughs, that is, doughs without a preferment, and as such, they can all be prepared and baked the same day. The six recipes cover a range of different styles and techniques: white, half wholemeal, and 100% wholemeal; wheat, rye, and spelt flours; doughs incorporating dairy, whole grains and seeds; and a dark malt bread that needs little in the way of kneading. Aside from the malt bread, which really needs to be proved and baked in a loaf tin, each dough can be used for a variety of bread forms.

The recipes can be prepared by hand or using a mixer, although I thoroughly recommend making bread by hand, at least to begin with, so that one acquires a feel for the dough and can gain the experience needed to adjust the recipe according to the properties of the specific flour used and prevailing environmental conditions.

All of the recipes are based on a moderately strong bread flour; for the white wheat flour, something in the range 12.5 to 13.5% protein. If using a stronger flour, a little more water may be needed to achieve the same results, and, conversely, if using a lower protein flour, the amount of water may need to be reduced. It is well worth finding a flour that you like — ideally a stoneground organic flour — and experimenting with the hydration of the dough to find the right amount for the specific flour used.

Yeast quantities are indicative only. A pinch of yeast will leaven the dough if given enough time, whilst increasing the amount will result in a faster rise, but at the cost of flavour. Kitchen scales are often rather poor at measuring such small amounts; one can instead use measuring spoons for the yeast, with the approximation of 3 g dried yeast per teaspoon. Thus, for the basic white dough, below, I would use around $1\frac{1}{3}$ teaspoons of yeast. By all means reduce the amount of yeast for a slower fermentation that will be beneficial for flavour. I use cold filtered water for my bread; using luke warm water, which is the norm, will reduce fermentation time a little. Timings are indicative only; room temperature will have a significant impact on fermentation and proving time. The dough should roughly double in volume during fermentation, then almost double again during the final prove, but test by feel during the prove so as not to over prove the dough.

The basic method is the same for several of these recipes. To avoid repetition, it is fully described for the basic white dough, below, then only any differences in approach noted in subsequent recipes.

5.1 Basic white dough

This recipe is for a basic white dough that can be used for anything from a sliced loaf to a baton or rolls. This is an ideal dough to practise on and develop a feel for the dough and the techniques required for effective mixing, kneading, folding, shaping, and baking that are fundamental to all of the remaining recipes. If one can master this, none of the recipes in the rest of this book should offer much difficulty.

I like to add a little rye to this otherwise white dough; it adds something to the texture, flavour, and colour of the finished bread. In the small proportion suggested, it has no significant detrimental effect on gluten development, but if preferred, this could be prepared with 100% white wheat flour instead. I typically prepare this sort of dough at around 70% hydration. One might wish to experiment with this, and consider reducing to perhaps around 65% if making in a tin for a simple white sliced loaf, where the larger holes of a more hydrated dough might be inconvenient.

The autolyse step, noted in the method, is somewhat optional. Personally, I like to give the dough a full hour to hydrate and for the enzymes to get to work, but this can be reduced to twenty minutes, or even ignored completely, although more effort will then be needed to develop the dough during kneading. I knead in two short sessions with a rest period in between, adding the salt just before the second kneading. I do not overwork the dough during kneading, but incorporate several folds during fermentation. This approach does require the baker to return to the dough periodically, so although there is little effort involved, this might not always be convenient for the home baker. If there is no time to put in the folds, then develop the dough fully during kneading, making sure that it is properly elastic before leaving to ferment.

Table 5.1: Basic white dough

Ingredient	g	%	Notes
white wheat flour	495	90	
wholemeal rye flour	55	10	
water	385	70	
salt	11	2	
yeast	4.1	0.75	
batch size (to suit 2 lb loaf tin, one boule or batard, or four batons)	950	172.75	

Method

- Measure the flours into a bowl or other suitable container.

- Add the water and mix well, then cover with a cloth and leave for twenty minutes to one hour — this is the autolyse step.

- Sprinkle the yeast on top of the dough and fold in, using the dough scraper to help as needed.

- Tip the dough out onto the worktop and knead for perhaps five minutes or so until it comes together as a smooth, consistent, dough.

- Turn over the bowl to cover the dough and leave to rest for ten minutes or so.

- Spread out the dough a little and sprinkle over the salt.

- Fold and work the dough to incorporate the salt, then continue to knead for another few minutes, until elastic.
- Form the dough into a ball, using a little flour if needed.
- Lightly flour the bowl, return the dough to the bowl, and cover with a cloth.
- Let the dough ferment for around two hours, folding the dough every 30 minutes.
- Remove the dough, divide and shape as desired, and prove for around one hour, until almost doubled in size.
- For batons:
  - One hour before baking, heat the oven to 250°C, preferably with a baking stone, or otherwise a heavy baking sheet. Place a heavy pan at the bottom of the oven.
  - When ready to bake, score the batons and transfer to the baking stone.
  - Add a splash of water to the pan to generate steam and bake for ten minutes before opening the oven door to allow excess steam to escape.
  - Reduce the temperature to 220°C and bake for a further ten to 15 minutes, depending on size.
- For a boule or batard:
  - One hour before baking, heat the oven to 250°C, preferably with a baking stone, or otherwise a heavy baking sheet. Place a heavy pan at the bottom of the oven.
  - When ready to bake, score the loaf and transfer to the baking stone.
  - Add a splash of water to the pan to generate steam and bake for ten minutes before opening the oven door to allow excess steam to escape.
  - Reduce the temperature to 220°C and bake for a further 20 to 30 minutes for a 500 g loaf or 25 to 35 minutes for a 1 kg loaf.
- For crusty rolls:
  - One hour before baking, heat the oven to 250°C, preferably with a baking stone, or otherwise a heavy baking sheet. Place a heavy pan at the bottom of the oven.
  - When ready to bake, score the rolls if desired and transfer to the baking stone, allowing space for expansion.
  - Add a splash of water to the pan to generate steam and bake for ten minutes before opening the oven door to allow excess steam to escape.
  - Reduce the temperature to 220°C and bake for a further ten minutes or so.
- For softer rolls:
  - One hour before baking, heat the oven to 200°C, preferably with a baking stone, or otherwise a heavy baking sheet. Place a heavy pan at the bottom of the oven.
  - When ready to bake, spray the surface of the rolls with a little water if desired,

then transfer to the baking stone, allowing space for expansion.

- Add a splash of water to the pan to generate steam and bake for ten minutes before opening the oven door to allow excess steam to escape.
- Bake for a further ten to 15 minutes.

• For a 2lb loaf tin:

- Half an hour before baking, heat the oven to 220°C. Place a heavy pan at the bottom of the oven.
- When ready to bake, place the loaf tin on the oven shelf.
- Add a splash of water to the pan to generate steam and bake for ten minutes before opening the oven door to allow excess steam to escape.
- Reduce the temperature to 200°C and bake for a further 30 to 45 minutes.

Basic white bread

5.2 Wholemeal and white wheat loaf

This recipe was created as a replacement for the ubiquitous supermarket sliced loaf that we always had in our freezer for making a quick slice of toast. I wanted the flavour and nutrition of some wholemeal flour but with a lighter texture, hence use a mixture of 50% white and 50% wholemeal. The recipe can be adapted, though, according to preference, bearing in mind that if increasing the amount of wholemeal flour, the water content should be increased also, and *vice versa*. Milk and butter are included in this dough for both their flavour and their tenderising effect. The result is an ideal loaf for slicing and toasting, with a fairly even, tender, crumb. It freezes well and can be toasted from frozen with good effect. Sized to suit a 2 lb loaf tin, this recipe also makes good rolls. Leave to cool completely before attempting to slice, and if freezing, do so as soon as possible.

Table 5.2: Wholemeal and white wheat loaf

Ingredient	g	%	Notes
white wheat flour	265	50	
wholemeal wheat flour	265	50	
water	170	32	
whole milk	239	45	
butter	27	5	
salt	10	2	
yeast	4	0.75	
batch size (to suit 2 lb loaf tin)	980	184.75	

Method

The method generally follows that for the basic white dough, above. It differs, though, in the preparation of the liquid ingredients. As milk contains glutathione, which can act to weaken the gluten, it is first scalded and then allowed to cool somewhat before adding to the dough. Place the milk and butter in a pan, and raise the temperature to 85°C. If a thermometer is not available, heat until small bubbles rise, but before coming to a full boil. Remove from the heat, allow to cool for 15 minutes or so, then add the cold water. The liquid, which should be no more than lukewarm, can then be added to the flours and matters proceed as for the basic white dough. The recipe is sized to suit one 2 lb loaf tin, but can equally be used to make rolls or other forms. If using a loaf tin, allow to prove until the dough rises just a few centimetres above the rim of the tin.

Wholemeal and white wheat loaf

5.3 Milk bread

When a soft white bread is needed, milk bread, or *pain au lait*, is a good candidate. Recipes vary somewhat, but commonly include milk and butter, along with additional sugar and sometimes also egg. For this recipe, I wanted the softness of a milk bread, but not the overt sweetness nor the richness brought by the sugar and egg. Hence, this recipe stops a little short of the classic pain au lait.

The moisture content in this dough is entirely derived from milk and butter. Whole milk is around 87% water so rather more is needed than if using water alone. The milk and butter add richness to the dough, bringing both fats and sugars. The result is a bread with a moist, tender crumb. This dough makes wonderful rolls, but is also well suited to proving and baking in a loaf tin for tender sliced bread.

Method

The method generally follows that for the basic white dough. Like the wholemeal and white wheat loaf, above, it contains milk, which is scalded before use. Place the milk and butter in a pan, and raise the temperature to 85°C. If a thermometer is not available, heat until small bubbles rise, but before coming to a full boil. Remove from the heat and allow to

Table 5.3: Milk bread

Ingredient	g	%	Notes
white wheat flour	500	100	
whole milk	435	87	
butter	50	10	
salt	10	2	
yeast	3.75	0.75	
batch size (to suit 2lb loaf tin)	999	199.75	

cool until just lukewarm before proceeding. The liquid can then be added to the flour and matters proceed as for the basic white dough. The dough will not be quite so elastic when kneaded, but should at least become fairly smooth and supple. The bread, whether formed as rolls or a loaf, is best baked gently, at no more than 200°C, to leave a tender crust.

Milk bread

5.4   Spelt bread

Spelt is an ancient relative of common wheat, and brings a delicious nutty flavour to any bread in which it is used. This recipe makes one of my wife's favourite rolls, reminding her of something her grandmother used to make. I usually make these with 100% wholemeal spelt. The result is very pleasant, but like any bread with a large amount of the germ, it is rather heavier than those made with white flour. The fairly high hydration of 75% is helpful in producing a good crumb, and one can lighten the bread further, if desired, by using some white spelt flour, where available, or substituting white wheat flour if preferred. As wholemeal flours absorb more water, any substitution with white flour may suggest an appropriate reduction in the hydration. For the method, refer to the basic white dough of Section 5.1.

Table 5.4: Spelt bread

Ingredient	g	%	Notes
wholemeal spelt flour	550	100	
water	413	75	
salt	11	2	
yeast	4.1	0.75	
batch size (one boule or batard)	*978*	*177.75*	

Spelt bread, baked in a *La Cloche* baking dome

5.5 Wholegrain bread

Grains and seeds can be added to bread for flavour, texture, and nutritional benefit. They do, though, require particular treatment, which is why I included this recipe in the book. This is not, perhaps, an ideal recipe for a novice, as practice is needed to adjust the hydration according to how the dough develops, and the dough is less easy to handle than a regular unseeded sort. This recipe produces a wet dough that might look, on first impression, to be unworkable. However, though wet, it is not unduly sticky, and can be worked, gently, on an unfloured surface, where a little patience will see the dough develop nicely.

Whilst one might get away with adding a small amount of certain tender seeds, such as linseed, to a dough without taking any special precautions, most grains and seeds do require changes in the approach. They offer several challenges: first, they can absorb large amounts of moisture, of the order of twice their own weight; second, they can be tough in the finished bread and unpleasant to chew on; and, finally, they physically damage the strands of gluten, cutting them through, and thus preventing a fully elastic dough from being developed.

The water absorption and tenderness of the grains and seeds is readily addressed by preparing a *soaker*. Recipes vary as to how long to soak and whether to soak in cold water, boiling water, or even to cook out the grains for some time. It rather depends on which grains and seeds are being considered, the harder sorts benefiting from soaking in hot water, and for some hours, preferably over night. Rather than over complicate matters, I soak all of the seeds

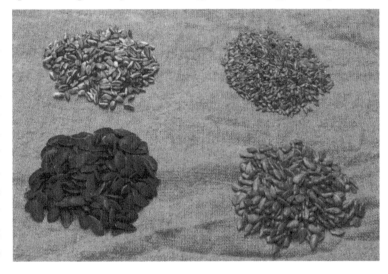

Whole grains and seeds; clockwise from top left: spelt berries, golden linseed, sunflower seeds, pumpkin seeds

and grains used in boiling water, for some hours, and typically over night, ready to add to the dough in the morning. Note that, in the table below, the final weight of the dough is only approximate. This is because the amount of water that the grains absorb is rather difficult to predict. Even when drained, the soaked seeds can be gloopy and tend to retain a certain amount of excess moisture, which makes the dough rather wet when they are added.

As for the tendency of grains to damage the gluten, one could develop the gluten first, and then mix in the grains. However, the soaked grains bring with them a certain amount of moisture, altering the characteristics of the dough, and are hard to work uniformly into a fully developed dough. The alternative is to add the grains at the beginning and work the sticky dough gently by hand so as not to break up the larger seeds, and rely on the fermentation and folding to complete the development of the gluten to a reasonable degree. Recipes may vary as to which approach to take; neither is ideal, but here I adopt the latter.

A wide range of seeds and grains can be used in bread. In this recipe I use equal amounts, by weight, of sunflower seeds, pumpkin seeds, golden linseed, and whole spelt grains. Other options include wheat and rye berries, oats, barley, millet, sesame and poppy seeds. One can also vary the total amount of grains added. If I am going to make such a bread, I like to make sure there are plenty of seeds and grains, so that they add much character to the flavour and texture of the finished loaf.

For this bread, I use a malted bread flour, which is essentially a brown flour, so having a reasonable amount of the wheat bran, with malted wheat flakes and malted barley. Various brands produce such a flour, although one may need to adjust the hydration to suit the particular flour used. I also add a little malt extract for the flavour and colour.

I prepare this bread with water only, but one could also use a proportion of scalded milk, bearing in mind that full fat milk is only around 87% water, and so increasing the amount to suit. A little butter might also be a suitable addition, although, again, I tend to prepare this bread without, and find the texture pleasant as it is.

Table 5.5: Wholegrain bread

Ingredient	g	%	Notes
soaker			
sunflower seeds	25	5.6	
pumpkin seeds	25	5.6	
whole spelt grains	25	5.6	
golden linseed	25	5.6	
water	300	n/a	
dough			
malted bread flour	450	100	
water	300	67	
malt extract	23	5	
salt	11	2.4	
yeast	3.4	0.75	
batch size (to suit 2 lb loaf tin)	c. 1 kg	197.55	

Method

- Prepare the soaker by placing the seeds and grains in a bowl.
- Boil the water for the soaker and pour over the seeds and grains.
- Allow to cool, then cover and leave to soak for several hours, ideally overnight.
- Place the flour and malt extract in a bowl.
- Drain the seeds, adding the liquid to the bowl, and top up to the required amount

with fresh water. At this stage it is sensible to withhold, say, 50 g of the water until after the seeds are mixed in and adjust afterwards.

- Add the seeds and mix well, adjusting the hydration, if necessary, to form a fairly wet dough.

- Cover with a cloth and leave for one hour.

- Proceed to develop the dough in the usual manner, adding the yeast, kneading, resting, adding the salt, then kneading again, until smooth and supple.

- Ferment for two hours or so, folding three times, at 30 minute intervals.

- Best proved and baked in a loaf tin.

Wholegrain bread

5.6 Malt bread

With this recipe I was caught between two traditions: the British malt bread, dark, sticky, and raisin studded, and perhaps more cake like than bread; and those from my wife's homeland of Finland, such as maalahden limppu or saaristolaisleipä, a bit less sweet and sticky, a little heavier, perhaps due to the common inclusion of rye flour and bran, and more distinctly bread like. A good example of either sort of malt bread can be delicious.

Recipes for the British sort often use baking soda, which no doubt contributes to the cake like structure, and the results are more of a sweet treat than a savoury bread. The Finnish sort, though, is much more a savoury bread, albeit with sweetness from malt and, often, molasses. Recipes vary widely, with little agreement even on the flour, which might include bran, oats, and barley in addition to wheat and rye flours. Buttermilk is common, but recipes for malt breads can be found with fruit juice, beer, and tea as part of the liquid component.

For this recipe, I have simplified matters somewhat. I use the same malted bread flour as for the wholegrain bread, above, which is essentially a brown flour, with some malted wheat flakes and malted barley, and then add some wholemeal rye flour. Milk and butter provide the fat and water content, and a combination of malt and molasses — or black treacle — brings the characteristic flavour and colour of malt bread. Malt breads are often markedly more sweet than this recipe. Although it contains a large amount of malt extract, this is not as sweet as one might expect — the malt extract used contains around 70% sugars, predominantly maltose, which tastes about one third as sweet as sucrose. From a quick straw poll of a small group of Finnish ladies, most liked the recipe as it is, one or two even suggested it could be a little less sweet, whilst a couple wanted more sweetness. To make a sweeter version one could replace some of the malt with honey. Quite a few recipes for malt bread include additional sugar, most often a brown sugar with its higher molasses content.

The dough is wet, sticky, and not something one would wish to knead. This is the ideal time to use a stand mixer, with beater attachment rather than dough hook, to mix and develop the dough a little before packing into loaf tins to ferment. Alternatively, it can be given a vigorous beating with a wooden spoon. There is no separate stage of shaping and proving. The result is more Finnish than British, but not an authentic representation of either. I do not add raisins to this bread, but there is no reason why various fruits or nuts could not be mixed into the dough.

The recipe is sized for a 2 lb loaf tin. The dough weight is reduced from that typical for this size of tin as it is lacking in structure and best not allowed to rise too much above the top of the tin during the bake.

Method

- Place the milk and butter in a pan, and raise the temperature to 85°C. If a thermometer is not available, heat until small bubbles rise, but before coming to a full boil. Remove from the heat.

- Stir the malt and molasses into the milk and butter mixture, and allow to cool until lukewarm.

- Place the flours in the bowl of a stand mixer, or mixing bowl if preparing by hand. Stir in the yeast, then the salt.

- Pour in the milk and butter and mix on low speed until combined, then turn up the speed and mix for a few minutes until the dough is smooth. It will not form up like normal dough and will remain loose and sticky; more like a thick batter. If working by hand, mix vigorously for a few minutes with a wooden spoon.

- Cover and allow to ferment for 30 minutes.
- Pack the dough into loaf tins, smoothing the top with the back of a spoon or spatula, wetting it if needed to prevent sticking.
- Cover and ferment for around three hours, when it should be well risen but still clear from the top of the pan.
- Bake at 190°C for around 40 minutes for a 2 lb loaf tin.
- Turn out of the tin and place on a wire rack to cool.

Table 5.6: Malt bread

Ingredient	g	%	Notes
malted bread flour	280	80	
wholemeal rye flour	70	20	
malt extract	105	30	
molasses	53	15	
milk	245	70	
butter	18	5	
salt	8	2.3	
yeast	3.5	1	
batch size (to suit 2 lb loaf tin)	783	223.3	

Malt bread

6. Flatbreads

The term flatbread can refer to any of a wide range of breads that are stretched, pressed, rolled, or otherwise formed into fairly flat loaves. Unleavened sorts were covered in Chapter 2, and griddle cakes leavened with baking soda in Chapter 3; this chapter considers a number of common sorts leavened with yeast: the oval shaped pitta bread, the tear shaped naan, a soft wrap, and the olive oil soaked focaccia. Flatbreads are often flavoured with such things as onions, cheese, herbs, olives, and so on, and the doughs covered here can be adapted to create a wide range of breads. I use the focaccia dough for garlic bread, pizza, and the Alsace dish known as *tarte flambée* or *flammkuchen*, depending which side of the French–German border one happens to be; recipes are described for all three. I cook the pitta and naan on a baking stone in a hot oven, but thin flatbreads of this sort can also be cooked on a griddle.

A strong bread flour gives flatbreads a pleasant chewy texture, and the elasticity to stretch without tearing, but such an elastic dough can be quite challenging to roll out, especially if making a thin pizza crust. A rest during shaping may be helpful in that regard, but a lengthy retardation of the dough is even better. With the doughs of the previous chapter, a high degree of elasticity is beneficial to keep their forms when shaped as boules, batards, batons, rolls, and so on, and during a long fermentation, factors such as enzyme activity will degrade the protein somewhat, resulting in doughs that relax rather too much after shaping. The doughs of the following chapter use preferments as a way to bring benefits of strength and, more importantly, flavour to the dough, where only a portion of the flour is fermented for an extended period. With these flatbread doughs, though, a lengthy fermentation of the whole dough is entirely appropriate. In this way, one may prepare a large batch of dough and bake in portions over the course of several days.

After they have fermented for an hour or two, reserve whatever may be needed for immediate use, gently degas and fold the remaining dough, put in a bowl, cover with film, and place in the refrigerator. The dough will continue to develop slowly, so allow plenty of room for expansion. It will be good for at least several days. Degas and fold the dough from time to time to keep it under control. Pizza dough, very elastic on the first day, will, after several days in the refrigerator, become much more extensible and more readily formed into a thin base. The depth of flavour, texture, and crust, will all be improved after a long fermentation, so dough can be prepared well ahead of time. My Bengali sister-in-law assures me that her mother always allowed her naan dough to rest for two days before baking, a recommendation with which I wholeheartedly concur. Allow refrigerated dough to return to room temperature before final shaping. Pizza dough can be divided into portions before refrigerating and this seems to be a common recommendation. I tend to just leave a large bowl of dough in the refrigerator, cutting off portions and preshaping as and when needed, then leaving to warm up before final shaping. I have seen it recommended to put the kneaded dough either directly in the refrigerator or give it just a short fermentation, say, half an hour at room temperature before refrigeration, the idea being that the fermentation is done at low temperature over the course of a couple of days. However, I generally allow time for the dough to rise properly at room temperature before folding and placing in the refrigerator to continue to develop. The dough is quite capable of rising several times before it becomes tired. In my experience, this approach yields an excellent dough after three days in the refrigerator.

The method for developing the doughs in this chapter proceeds much along the same lines as those of the previous chapter. They may be prepared by hand with an autoylse step and kneaded as described for the basic white dough of Section 5.1. These doughs in particular should be quite elastic, so I generally develop the gluten fairly well through kneading, more so than with those of the previous chapter. Although I generally prefer to work dough by hand, I will sometimes use a stand mixer for these recipes, especially if making a large batch of pizza dough.

6.1   Pitta

This dough can be used as the basis for a variety of flatbreads, as well as the classic pitta. I generally prefer white flour for pitta bread, but one can use wholemeal flour or a combination, increasing the water content as needed. Good hydration is important with pitta to get the bread to puff up when cooked and provide the pocket between the top and bottom crusts that is often opened up and stuffed. If not intending to stuff the pitta, the dough can be docked, that is, pierced through with a fork or knife, to prevent excessive puffing up. Unless brushing with butter or oil, warm pitta bread can be wrapped in a cloth once baked, where the residual steam will help to keep it soft. For a large pitta, scale the portions at around 100 g.

Table 6.1: Pitta bread

Ingredient	g	%	Notes
white wheat flour	375	100	
water	250	67	
olive oil	19	5	
salt	7.5	2	
yeast	2.8	0.75	
batch size (approx. 6 large pitta breads)	654	174.75	

Method

Develop the dough, either by hand or machine, in the usual way — see Section 5.1 — then proceed as follows:

- Let the dough ferment for two or three hours.

- Remove the dough and divide and shape approximately into balls.
- Stretch or roll out on a lightly floured surface to around ½ cm in thickness, forming either the classic elongated form or rounds, as preferred.
- Let the dough rest for 20 minutes or so.
- Half an hour before baking, heat the oven to 220°C, preferably with a baking stone, or otherwise a heavy baking sheet.
- When ready to bake, transfer the pitta bread to the baking stone and bake for around seven to eight minutes, until puffed and just beginning to colour.

Pitta bread

6.2 Naan

Naan is a classic flatbread originating from India, traditionally cooked in the searing heat of a tandoor — a somewhat vase shaped, often wood or charcoal fired, clay oven — where it cooks in moments. It should be light and fluffy inside with a golden crust that is not unduly hard. Like pizza, the oven does make a difference in how the bread cooks, and the tandoor undoubtedly is the right tool for the job, capable of reaching temperatures of more than

200°C above that of a domestic oven. However, although making a tandoor at home is not too difficult, naan can be cooked successfully in a hot oven, especially with the benefit of a baking stone.

Recipes for naan vary widely. Many are leavened with baking soda, but I much prefer to use yeast; the texture when using baking soda is, in my view, quite wrong for this sort of bread. Yoghurt is a common addition. It provides the required acidity if leavening with baking soda, but is also included in many versions that are leavened with yeast. Some dairy is certainly useful in achieving the desired texture. Yoghurt, being made simply by adding a suitable culture to milk, is, like milk, largely water, so in this recipe a large portion of the water content is provided by the yoghurt. The recipe assumes an ordinary plain yoghurt, not strained or otherwise thickened. The dough can be used the same day as it is prepared, after a proper fermentation, but is markedly improved with a couple of days in the refrigerator.

Naan is often flavoured with various herbs, spices, garlic, and so on, and sometimes stuffed with nuts, spiced meat, or other fillings. Kalonji seeds are a fairly common addition, and can be added to the dough or sprinkled on the surface. I often include them, and also a sprinkling of chopped coriander, after brushing with melted butter.

Table 6.2: Naan bread

Ingredient	g	%	Notes
white wheat flour	350	100	
water	105	30	
butter	35	10	
yoghurt	158	45	
salt	7	2	
yeast	2.6	0.75	
batch size (4 large naan)	658	187.75	

Method

Making naan is little different from the pitta breads above. When mixing, melt the butter and stir into the yoghurt before adding to the dry ingredients. Proceed to develop the dough as usual. Allow the dough to ferment for around three hours, at which time it may be divided and rolled out into rounds or the traditional tear shape. Alternatively, gently degas, fold the dough, and place in the refrigerator for a day or two, during which time the dough will continue to develop slowly.

The naan bread can be cooked as soon as it has been shaped, although there may be something to be gained from allowing the dough to rest for a while. Dock the dough in half a dozen places, that is, pierce the dough through, using a sharp knife or fork, to prevent large areas from puffing up; some puffing up is beneficial, but this is not supposed to open up like a pitta. Naan can be baked in a hot oven, around 250°C, preferably with the benefit of a baking stone, for around six minutes, which is my preferred method. Alternatively, they can be cooked on a hot griddle for a few minutes on each side. Best served immediately, brushed with melted butter.

Naan bread

6.3 Soft wrap

From time to time we have need of a soft wrap, along the lines of the wheat tortillas that are readily available from the supermarket. These are ideal for various purposes, but the commercial versions, although convenient, are far from fresh and this is reflected in the somewhat dull and stale taste.

Traditional tortillas, made from fine ground nixtamalised corn, are unleavened — see Section 2.2, but these are quite different from the soft wheat, or largely wheat, versions, the majority of which are leavened with baking soda. For my home made soft wrap I prefer to use yeast rather than baking powder as the flavour and texture developed from fermentation are much better. To help produce a soft dough the water in this recipe is added to the flour whilst hot, an interesting method that appears to be in use in parts of East Asia and, in the context of rye breads, Scandinavia. More usually applied to a portion of the flour, the hot water cooks out the starches, producing a soft dough, although not as elastic as it might otherwise be. The amount of water used is increased over a normal dough, and even at the suggested hydration, the dough may still be a little stiff to mix. Wraps are often made entirely with white wheat flour, but various amounts of wholemeal wheat can be used according to preference, increasing the water if necessary to keep a soft and supple dough.

Table 6.3: Soft wrap

Ingredient	g	%	Notes
white wheat flour	300	100	
water	240	80	
olive oil	30	10	
salt	6	2	
yeast	2.25	0.75	
batch size (makes approx. 8 wraps)	578	192.75	

Soft wrap

Method

The dough is developed following the usual method except that, in the first instance, the water is brought to a boil before adding to the flour and olive oil. This is then mixed and left to stand for one hour, before proceeding. The dough will feel quite different and will not be as smooth and elastic as one might expect, although during fermentation it will change and begin to feel more like a conventional dough again. If working by hand, knead it well, but do not be unduly concerned about elasticity. Fold the dough numerous times during fermentation. The dough should ferment for several hours after which it can be used or refrigerated as needed.

The dough — allowed to return to room temperature if it has been refrigerated — should be divided into pieces of around 60 to 70 g and rolled out on a floured worktop until about as thin as is practical. Shake off the excess flour needed to roll them out and cook in a heavy pan over a medium–high heat for a minute or so on each side until lightly coloured. Wrap in a cloth whilst still warm to keep them soft.

6.4   Focaccia

Focaccia is a delicious, fairly flat, bread, flavoured with copious amounts of olive oil and seasoned generously with coarse salt, and often rosemary and garlic. It is the Italian equivalent of the French *fougasse*, although that tends to be made with little or no added fat. I generally use a preferment when making fougasse, see Section 7.7, to ensure that the white dough has a great flavour, but with focaccia, which gets so much flavour from the oil rich crust, I use this straight dough.

Focaccia can vary greatly in thickness and in texture, from the thin Tuscan *schiacciata* to the thick doughy versions that one can find in our supermarkets. The latter is not, to my mind, proper focaccia, nor, to my taste, a pleasant experience at all. The texture and the crust are both quite wrong. I prefer something thinner, with a generous amount of olive oil, a thin but crisp and golden crust, and light flavoursome interior that is not at all doughy.

This focaccia dough is quite versatile; I use the same recipe to make garlic bread, pizza, and tarte flambée. I often add some finely chopped rosemary to the dough when making focaccia, but this is optional, and I do not usually add it when making pizza. Semolina is a common addition to pizza dough, and works equally well in the focaccia, but both can be prepared with entirely white wheat flour if preferred. A high gluten content is often sought for pizza dough, and works well for focaccia, helping to develop a desirable chewy texture. Whilst pizza dough certainly benefits from several days of slow development in the refrigerator, I tend to make focaccia the same day, although in this case the elasticity of the dough makes it a little tricky to stretch out. By all means leave for a day or two, after which it will be easier to work.

For the authentic finish, do not skimp on the olive oil; it is where the bread gets much of its flavour and the delicious golden crust from. Note that I reduce the amount of salt slightly in the dough from the usual 2%, as it is traditionally sprinkled with lots of coarse salt.

Method

Focaccia is proved and baked on baking sheets. Mine are 10×15 inch or approximately 25×38 cm, for which the suggested batch size will make two full trays, but one can scale to suit whatever trays are available. Develop the dough, either by hand or machine, then proceed as follows:

- Let the dough ferment for two to three hours, folding several times.
- Remove the dough and divide into portions to suit available baking sheets.
- Spread a thin layer of olive oil on the baking sheets.
- Place each portion of dough on a baking sheet and stretch, pull, and prod the dough to spread it out until the tray is more or less filled, which should result in dough of around 1½ cm in thickness.
- Cover and leave to prove for half an hour to one hour.
- Half an hour before baking, heat the oven to 220°C.
- When ready to bake, use fingers to dimple the dough, drizzle with olive oil and sprinkle with plenty of coarse sea salt.
- Bake for around 20 to 25 minutes, until a crisp golden crust is formed.
- Remove from the trays and cool on a wire rack.

Table 6.4: Focaccia

Ingredient	g	%	Notes
white wheat flour	600	80	
semolina	150	'20	
water	488	65	
olive oil	75	10	
chopped rosemary (optional)	12	1.6	
salt	13	1.75	
yeast	5.6	0.75	
batch size (makes two trays)	1344	179.1	

Variations

The classic focaccia is delicious, but there are many variations; some authentic sorts are described below. Baking times may need to be extended by five minutes or so for those with thick toppings.

- *Garlic and rosemary focaccia.* Prior to baking, place thin slices of garlic in the dimples, and sprinkle with rosemary leaves.

- *Onion focaccia.* One can add finely sliced raw onions to the top, but I prefer to sauté them first in a little olive oil for five minutes or so to soften, seasoning with salt, black pepper, and a pinch of sugar, and adding some rosemary and sliced garlic near the end of cooking. The onions are then spread on top of the focaccia before baking.

- *Potato focaccia.* A layer of finely sliced potatoes can be spread on top of the dough, brushed with olive oil and sprinkled with salt, and perhaps some rosemary.

- *Courgette focaccia.* Courgettes can be used to top the focaccia, but are perhaps best salted first. Slice fairly thinly, place in a bowl, sprinkle with salt, and leave for at least half an hour for the salt to draw out some of the excess moisture. Drain, pat dry, and toss in a little olive oil before spreading out on top of the dough.

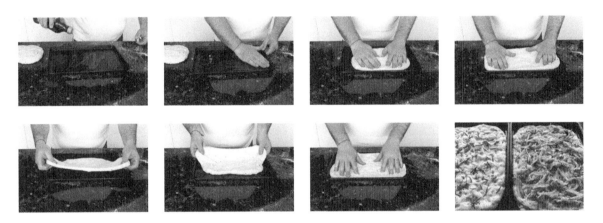

Shaping the focaccia

6.5 Garlic bread

Garlic bread can be prepared with various sorts of bread. Often a 'fake' baguette is used — that is, something vaguely baguette shaped but with the rather poor crust, overly dense texture, and mediocre flavour from which so many of our baguette substitutes suffer. Several of the recipes in this book could be used, but one of the best is a garlic flatbread prepared quickly and easily using the focaccia dough, above. Like pizza, below, portions can be scaled at around 165 g. This makes a good sized garlic bread that will readily fit on a baking stone, not to mention an ordinary dinner plate. The batch size above will produce around eight such garlic breads, or more if using smaller portions; scale the quantities to suit, or store any left over dough in the refrigerator to develop slowly, allowing it to come up to room temperature before using.

Prepare a garlic butter by taking 100 g butter, 2 or 3 cloves of garlic, and a sprig of rosemary — other herbs can be used if preferred, parsley being a more common option.

Focaccia

Finely chop the rosemary, and mince the garlic with a little coarse salt. Place the ingredients in a small pan and warm over a low heat until the butter has melted and the garlic just begins to cook, but do not allow either the garlic or the butter to colour. Season with black pepper and set aside for the flavour to develop. This can be prepared ahead of time and refrigerated until needed.

Turn the oven to its hottest setting; my ovens go to 275°C, but 250°C would still be sufficient. A baking stone is highly recommended to achieve great results with this recipe, but a heavy duty baking sheet can be used as an alternative. Heat the oven and baking stone or sheet for an hour before baking.

Flour the worktop lightly to prevent sticking. A mixture of white flour and semolina works well for this purpose. Divide the dough into portions and shape into balls. One at a time, or more if making smaller portions or using more than one oven, roll out the dough thinly, or by all means employ the various pressing, slapping, and tossing techniques of the pizzeria. My dough is never entirely circular, and it really does not matter; indeed a rustic form is quite attractive. Dock the dough, that is, pierce the dough through, with a fork or knife, in a few places, to prevent excessive puffing of the dough. It should bubble up, but one does not want a huge pocket to appear.

Dust a peel with semolina, or, if no peel is available, use the reverse side of a baking sheet.

80

Spread the dough out on the peel and slide onto the heated baking stone. The cooking time will depend on oven temperature and thickness of dough, but should be around four or five minutes. Bake until the bread picks up a little colour; one can vary this according to taste, allowing it to become quite crisp, or taking it whilst still rather soft and chewy. Meanwhile, warm the garlic butter until melted through.

Once cooked, remove the bread, brush generously with the melted garlic butter, and serve immediately. It is particularly good finished with a fine grating of parmesan cheese.

Garlic bread

6.6 Pizza

Pizza, prepared with some care, can be absolutely delicious, but it is also a much abused dish. Poor quality, doughy crusts, a nasty tomato sauce, overly topped so that both the topping and the top layer of dough stay wet and soggy, are just some of the crimes committed against this Italian classic. The secrets to great home cooked pizza lie in: getting the oven properly hot before cooking and using a baking stone; a good dough, properly fermented to give the right chewy texture; a good tomato sauce; and, carefully considered toppings, sparsely decorating the pizza so as not to prevent the bread from cooking. With good pizza, it is still the bread that is the star of the dish.

Whilst the heat of a wood fired pizza oven can cook a perfect pizza in just a minute or two, a domestic oven cannot achieve nearly the same sort of temperatures. However, good pizza can still be made at home. A baking stone is almost essential in trying to achieve a crisp, thin, crust. It is a modest investment for the benefit it brings, not just to pizza, but to all sorts of bread, and I highly recommend buying one. Many are made in round shapes, and referred to as pizza stones, but these are not, to my mind, a good idea. I prefer the rectangular sort, sized to fill a standard oven rack. This gives the most flexibility when making pizza and bread. The baking stone and oven should be heated to their hottest setting for around an hour before cooking; this is 275°C for my ovens, but 250°C would still work, albeit with slightly longer cooking times.

The focaccia dough above makes great pizza. It can be prepared ahead; in fact, it benefits from an extended fermentation in the refrigerator and can be used for several days; see the introductory notes to this chapter for discussion of refrigeration. The results are excellent after three days of retardation, when the dough will be far more readily shaped and will bring excellent flavour and characterful crust to the pizza. As with the garlic bread, above, I scale the portions at around 165 g, so the batch size given in the focaccia recipe will yield eight pizzas. The dough should be rolled out thinly on a worktop dusted with a mixture of flour and semolina to prevent sticking, the semolina contributing somewhat to the finish of the crust. Place the rolled out dough on a peel or the reverse side of a baking sheet dusted with plenty of semolina so that the pizza can be transferred to the oven with ease. Pizza does not have to be perfectly round; mine seldom are, and I like the rustic look. Spread with a thin layer of tomato sauce, leaving clear a couple of centimetres around the edge of the pizza. Sprinkle with the desired toppings, then bake for around 7 minutes at 275°C, or a little longer if the maximum oven temperature is lower than this, until the base is crisp and the toppings golden and bubbling.

There appear to be different opinions on the tomato sauce. Some suggest that a can of crushed tomatoes or jar of passata is suitable as it comes, whilst I prefer to remove a fair bit of the moisture content first. The domestic oven does not, in my view, get sufficiently hot to cope with too much moisture in the topping of the pizza. One can simply simmer the tomatoes first, to reduce them to a thick consistency. However, I like to first sauté a little fresh chilli in some olive oil, then add chopped garlic and rosemary, before putting in the tomatoes. Season with salt, black pepper, and a pinch of sugar to taste. I often use fresh tomatoes, when I have them from the garden, and simmer them for some hours, but three 400 g cans of chopped tomatoes should cook down nicely to provide enough for eight pizzas, with any left over sauce being ideal to dress some pasta.

On the subject of toppings, one should try to avoid anything particularly wet and also avoid dressing with a large amount of cheese and other toppings as these prevent steam escaping and lead to an unpleasant soggy layer of dough under the toppings. Genuine Italian pizza is dressed with care, using just a small amount of well considered, good quality, ingredients. A modest amount of cheese will melt and spread out to cover a pizza, so a thick layer is not needed. Whilst fresh mozzarella may be a nice addition, and may bake successfully in the heat of a pizza oven, it is very wet, so I prefer to avoid it. If you do want to use fresh mozzarella, slice it well ahead of time and allow the excess moisture to drain, blotting it thoroughly before putting on the pizza. Similarly, if using vegetables with a high moisture content, such as courgettes or aubergines, these can be sliced and salted a little before hand to draw out some of their excess moisture. Partially cooking some ingredients may also help to ensure excess moisture is removed before baking. When in Italy, my favourite toppings are small pieces of spicy sausage with finely sliced red onions, and salami with a few slices of grilled peppers, but there is an almost limitless range of possibilities.

Pizza

6.7 Tarte flambée or flammkuchen

Tarte flambée or flammkuchen is an Alsatian dish closely resembling pizza. A thin crust is spread with soft cheese and/or crème fraîche, topped with onions and bacon, and cooked until golden. I dare say there is a more authentic dough formulation, but I make mine using exactly the same focaccia dough that I use for pizza. Whilst finely sliced onions and bacon can be added directly, I prefer to sauté them first, to make sure that the bacon gets cooked properly and to soften the onions. The quantities below should provide for four portions.

Tarte flambée

Ingredients

- 250 g streaky bacon or lardons
- 300 g shallots
- 200 ml crème fraîche
- 200 g soft cheese
- 1 egg yolk
- olive oil
- nutmeg
- sugar
- salt
- black pepper

Method

- One hour before baking, heat the oven to its hottest setting, preferably with a baking stone, or otherwise a heavy baking sheet.
- Finely slice the shallots and sauté in a little olive oil for a few minutes, until softened but not browned, seasoning with salt and pepper and a pinch of sugar.
- Slice the streaky bacon and sauté until cooked through but not browned.

84

- Mix the crème fraîche and soft cheese, and beat in the egg yolk.
- Season the cheese mixture with a generous amount of black pepper, a little salt, and a grating of nutmeg.
- Dust a peel or the reverse side of a baking sheet with semolina.
- Form the dough into a round or rectangular shape, as if making pizza, and place on the peel.
- Spread some of the crème fraîche mixture over the dough, then sprinkle with some of the onions and bacon.
- Transfer the tarte to the hot baking stone or baking sheet and cook for around 7 or 8 minutes, until crisp underneath and golden brown and bubbling on top.

7. Preferments

The two previous chapters provided various recipes for so-called straight or direct doughs. These can provide loaves of bread with good texture and flavour, especially if the amount of yeast is not excessive and they are allowed plenty of time to ferment and prove. To improve the flavour and texture further, a longer process is needed. For the flatbreads of Chapter 6, this can be achieved through lengthy retardation in the refrigerator. For other forms of bread, this is not ideal due to the degrading of the protein over time. This is where preferments come in. Simply, a portion of the flour, water, and a little yeast, is mixed and allowed to ferment for some hours, often overnight. This long ferment brings benefits of strength to the dough and aroma and flavour to the bread, both at least in part attributed to the acids that develop through bacterial action that otherwise has too little time to happen. The result is bread with a great chewy texture and wonderful flavour that just cannot be obtained with a straight dough. Keeping qualities may also be improved.

Making bread with a preferment is no more difficult than the direct method, it just takes a little time. The breads of the previous two chapters may, of course, be readily adapted to use preferments, but it is also useful to have an array of recipes to hand so that one can produce good bread even if limited time is available. I tend to use preferments particularly for white breads, where they help extract the most flavour from the white wheat flour. Aside from the preparation of the preferment, the process also varies in that a lengthy autolyse step is not so often included. The most common sort of preferment is made with equal weights of flour and water and, most often, this does not leave sufficient water to properly hydrate the remaining flour. However, the inclusion of the preferment also has the effect of markedly reducing the kneading required as the gluten is already partly developed and the dough comes together remarkably quickly. Although the longer autolyse is absent, I do find that allowing the dough to stand for up to twenty minutes is still beneficial. I do not leave it any longer than this, though, as the yeast is active in the mixture.

7.1 Types of preferment

A preferment is any sort of flour and water mixture fermented for some time before being added to the dough mixture. The proportion of the overall flour weight of a recipe that is prefermented is quite variable, but is often in the range 20 to 40%. Preferments go by various names, amongst which common sorts are *pâte fermentée*, *poolish*, and *biga*. *Pâte fermentée* is simply old dough, left over from a previous batch of dough, or made for the purpose. It contains all of the dough's ingredients, including any salt added, and thus differs from other forms of preferment. The dough can be refrigerated after fermentation and used within the next day or two.

Poolish is, perhaps, the most common preferment. It is typically made from equal quantities, by weight, of flour and water, with a small amount of yeast. Poolish is ideal for adding flavour to baguette dough and others where extensibility is important. A biga is similar, and, although it seems to vary somewhat in the ratio of flour to water, generally appears to be of lower hydration than poolish, perhaps around 60%.

The effect of the differences in hydration is not immediately obvious, nor, perhaps, of such great consequence to the home baker. Both poolish and biga will contribute strength and flavour. A biga will tend to bring more strength to the dough, which may not be ideal for those breads where an overly strong dough would be difficult to shape. The poolish, though, with its higher hydration, will encourage more enzyme, yeast, and bacterial activity. It will not keep in optimum condition for as long as a biga and one can more readily over ferment a poolish.

Whether using a biga or poolish, there is an optimum point during the fermentation at which one would like to incorporate it into the final dough. The mixture will rise during fermentation, forming an airy texture and a domed top. Ideally, one would use it at the point of maximum expansion or just as it starts to collapse. Allowing it to ferment for too long, though, is detrimental to dough strength. Despite this, in practice, I have found both poolish and biga to be quite forgiving, and good results easy to achieve. The rate of fermentation is affected by the temperature, so the amount of yeast and/or the fermentation time may need to be adjusted to suit conditions. The water content can also be influential; thus one might use a little more yeast in a biga than a poolish if fermented over the same period.

The same sorts of figures are quoted in many sources, suggesting a percentage of dried yeast of around 0.25% of flour weight for a ferment of eight hours reducing to around 0.15% for 12 hours. As I generally begin with cold water and the room temperature can fall markedly during an overnight fermentation, I tend to increase the amount of yeast somewhat. Nonetheless, the quantities involved are rather small, and for baking a few loaves at home, it is difficult to measure accurately. I often measure, then, not by weight but using an approximate conversion of around 3 g per teaspoon of dried yeast. For a preferment with 200 g of flour, this equates to something around ¼ teaspoon of yeast.

Poolish: after mixing (left), and after fermentation (right)

7.2 Baguette

The baguette that I have in mind here, known in France as *baguette de tradition*, is a wonderful bread, full of aroma and flavour, with a rich golden crust and open texture, beloved of locals and tourists alike. It is a far cry from the so-called 'French stick' so often served up here, which often has a poor, pale looking crust, lacks flavour, and has a more uniform crumb with a much more dense and doughy texture. The baguette de tradition française is made to the highest standards, which are protected by law. Of all breads, there is a great deal of mastery required to prepare the perfect baguette, from the development of the dough, to the shaping and scoring, and developing a good crust during the bake. Nonetheless, the home baker can achieve a good quality baguette, far superior in flavour and texture to that generally available here, albeit of rather shorter stature — perhaps better referred to as a baton — the domestic oven generally not being able to take such a long loaf.

Hydration is important in baguette dough, to achieve the open texture and great oven bounce, and one might wish to experiment with the formula to push this up. I would not prepare the dough with less than 70% hydration, and suggest 75% in the formula below. One can prepare a baguette with a straight dough, with a preferment, or a sourdough culture. I like to make mine with a preferment, specifically a poolish, made from equal amounts, by weight, of flour and water.

A couche is the most convenient way of laying out the bread to prove; either a length of couche fabric specifically intended for the purpose, or a couple of linen tea towels. The couche should be well floured before use, as the dough will tend to remain a little sticky even when shaped. A baguette might be scaled at 350 g or more, but as mine are somewhat shorter, I scale at around 250 to 300 g. The portion should be adjusted to suit the size of baking stone or sheet used to bake and the desired diameter of the finished bread. I sometimes use smaller portions of dough, rolling them to the same length to produce a particularly thin version, akin to that known as *ficelle*. In even smaller portions, say, around 70 g, this recipe makes excellent crusty rolls, which I would tend to form like a small batard.

Method

- Combine the preferment ingredients in a bowl and mix well.
- Cover and leave to ferment for around ten to 12 hours.
- Place the dough ingredients, except for the salt, in a bowl and add the preferment.
- Mix well then cover and leave to stand for 20 minutes.
- Tip the dough out onto the worktop and knead for a few minutes until the dough starts to come together.
- Turn over the bowl to cover the dough and leave for ten minutes or so.
- Spread the dough a little and sprinkle over the salt.
- Fold and work the dough to incorporate the salt, then continue to knead for another

Table 7.1: Baguette

Ingredient	g	%	Notes
preferment			
white wheat flour	225	43	
water	225	43	
yeast	0.8	0.15	
dough			
white wheat flour	300	57	
water	168	32	
salt	10.5	2	
yeast	3.1	0.6	
batch size (3 or 4 batons)	*932*	*177.75*	
overall formula			
white wheat flour	**525**	**100**	
water	**393**	**75**	
salt	**10.5**	**2**	
yeast	**3.9**	**0.75**	

Baguette

few minutes, until fairly smooth and elastic.

- Form the dough into a ball, using a little flour if needed.

- Lightly flour the bowl, return the dough to the bowl, and cover with a cloth.

- Let the dough ferment for two to three hours, folding the dough three times at 30 minute intervals.

- Lightly flour the worktop and tip out the dough.

- Divide into portions, gently degas, and shape into batons. If the dough is too tight to shape without tearing, allow to sit for a few minutes before shaping.

- Lay the batons on well floured couche, folding the couche to separate each baton. Place either seam side down, or up, but keep note of where the seam is to ensure that it is placed down when baked.

- Cover and allow to prove for around 60 minutes, being careful not to allow the dough to over prove.

- Meanwhile, heat the oven to 250°C, preferably with a baking stone, or otherwise a heavy baking sheet. Place a heavy pan at the bottom of the oven.

- When ready to bake, use a sharp blade to score each baton, with several slashes on a slight angle along the centre line of the baton.

- Use a peel or the reverse side of a baking sheet to transfer the batons to the oven.

- Add a splash of water to the pan to generate steam and bake for ten minutes before opening the oven door to allow excess steam to escape.

- Reduce the temperature to 220°C and bake for a further ten to 15 minutes, until the crust is a rich golden colour.

7.3   Pain de campagne

Although I make several breads, such as baguette, ciabatta, focaccia, and fougasse, entirely with white wheat flour, for an ordinary white dough I most often add a small amount of rye flour, around 10 to 15%. In such a proportion it has little negative effect on the density of the bread, but adds something to the flavour and texture. My basic dough thus gravitated towards something akin to *pain de campagne*, a rustic French country bread, made with white wheat flour with the addition of some wholemeal wheat and/or rye flour. Such bread may be made using a preferment or a sourdough culture—recipes are provided for both forms; see Section 8.5 for the sourdough version. The amount of wholemeal wheat and/or rye can be varied, although the hydration of the dough may need to be adjusted accordingly as rye absorbs more moisture than wheat, and wholemeal wheat more than white wheat flour. This recipe is sized for preparing a boule or batard of about 1 kg. The same recipe can, of course, be prepared for smaller or larger loaves, and also produces a tasty roll.

Method

The method proceeds as for the baguettes above, up to the point of shaping.

- Divide into portions as necessary, gently degas, and shape into boules or batards.
- Shaped loaves are ideally placed on the reverse side of well floured baking sheets to be readily transferred to the oven.
- Cover and allow to prove for around 60 to 90 minutes.
- Meanwhile, heat the oven to 250°C, preferably with a baking stone, or otherwise a heavy baking sheet. Place a heavy pan at the bottom of the oven.
- Use a sharp blade to score each loaf then transfer to the oven.
- Add a splash of water to the pan to generate steam and bake for ten minutes before opening the oven door to allow excess steam to escape.
- Reduce the temperature to 220°C and bake until the crust is a rich golden colour and the loaf cooked through. For a 1 kg boule or batard this should take another 25 to 35 minutes.

Table 7.2: Pain de campagne

Ingredient	g	%	Notes
preferment			
white wheat flour	200	33	
water	160	27	
yeast	0.7	0.12	
dough			
white wheat flour	220	37	
wholemeal wheat flour	90	15	
wholemeal rye flour	90	15	
water	278	46	
salt	12	2	
yeast	3	0.5	
batch size (one large loaf)	1054	175.62	
overall formula			
white wheat flour	420	70	
wholemeal wheat flour	90	15	
wholemeal rye flour	90	15	
water	438	73	
salt	12	2	
yeast	3.7	0.62	

Pain de campagne (top), rye and caraway (bottom)

7.4 Rye and caraway

The distinctive, slightly bitter, aniseed flavour of caraway seeds is often paired with rye bread. This recipe makes a light rye loaf, with a lot of character imparted by the 25% rye flour, which is prefermented to develop the distinctive rye aroma and flavour. Caraway has a strong flavour; reduce the quantity if desired, or leave it out entirely for a plain rye bread. A little molasses is also added for flavour and colour, but again could be omitted if preferred. Wholemeal rye flour absorbs a lot of water — even at 100% hydration, the poolish will end up quite stiff after the flour has had time to soak up the moisture.

The method proceeds as for the pain de campagne above. The main fermentation should take around two hours and the proving not much more than one hour. This bread is ideal formed into a batard, or then proved and baked in a 2 lb loaf tin. Refer to Section 4.8 for baking temperatures and times for different forms.

Table 7.3: Rye and caraway

Ingredient	g	%	Notes
preferment			
wholemeal rye flour	125	25	
water	125	25	
yeast	0.4	0.08	
dough			
white wheat flour	375	75	
water	230	46	
molasses	25	5	
caraway seeds	5.5 (2 tsp)	1.1	
salt	10	2	
yeast	2.8	0.56	
batch size (2 lb loaf tin or one batard)	899	179.74	
overall formula			
white wheat flour	375	75	
wholemeal rye flour	125	25	
water	355	71	
molasses	25	5	
caraway seeds	5.5	1.1	
salt	10	2	
yeast	3.2	0.64	

7.5 Semolina bread

Semolina is made from the hard durum wheat most commonly associated with pasta and couscous. It is often included in recipes for pizza dough, where it contributes to the formation of a good crust. I use a lot of semolina to flour baking sheets, peels, and so on, to prevent dough from sticking and to help transfer loaves to the oven. Although its appearance in bread recipes is less common, some bread is made with semolina, notably in southern Italy, a well known example being the regional speciality *pane di Altamura*. As I experimented with the formulation of my focaccia and pizza dough, I wondered about the effect of using a larger proportion of semolina. Thus began a series of experiments exploring the effect of incorporating semolina into an otherwise white dough, along with the addition of a little olive oil.

Semolina is known for producing a great crust. I had also read that it can result in a more dense and chewy texture, but this is not my experience. I began with one third semolina, using 200 g white bread flour for the preferment, a further 200 g in the main dough, along with 200 g of semolina. This produced a very nice loaf, with a great crust, excellent rise, and a wonderfully soft interior, with a fairly open crumb. I increased the proportion of semolina until I was using only semolina; the texture was not markedly changed — it remained distinctly soft, but with the golden yellow colour of the semolina, and an excellent flavour.

This recipe works well at one third semolina, and I would consider adding a little semolina to any recipe where a good crust is desired. The table presents the 100% semolina version.

Table 7.4: Semolina bread

Ingredient	g	%	Notes
preferment			
semolina	200	33	
water	160	27	
yeast	0.7	0.12	
dough			
semolina	400	67	
water	240	40	
olive oil	30	5	
salt	12	2	
yeast	3	0.5	
batch size (one batard)	1046	174.62	
overall formula			
semolina	600	15	
water	400	67	
olive oil	30	5	
salt	12	2	
yeast	3.7	0.62	

It is, to my mind, the perfect bread for a bacon butty or for lightly toasting and spreading with marmalade. In fact, this experiment has produced one of my favourite breads.

Semolina is rather coarse, but once hydrated, becomes soft and supple. The dough is easy to work and handle — perhaps my favourite of all doughs in this book. It has good strength, holding its shape well and with a good rise during baking. The method proceeds exactly as for the pain de campagne, although whereas I generally shape the pain de campagne as a boule, I prefer this loaf as a batard, which gives nice large slices from the centre of the loaf.

Semolina bread

7.6 Ciabatta

It may be surprising to find that ciabatta, one of the the most well known of Italian breads, is a rather modern creation, the original apparently developed in 1982 by Arnaldo Cavallari of Adria, in the Veneto region of Italy, as an alternative to the increasingly popular French baguette. It has, in a short space of time, spread far and wide, and established itself as a popular bread for a continental style sandwich, or *panino*. There are now many different recipes carrying the ciabatta label; some use a preferment, others do not, some are very wet doughs, others only moderately so, some require kneading, whilst some require little more than a few folds, and others still adopt a slow fermentation and a no-knead approach.

A good ciabatta is characterised by: a rustic, fairly flat form, with wrinkled floury surface; a thin crust, of a light golden colour, but not particularly hard; an open crumb with large and irregular holes; great flavour and somewhat chewy texture. To achieve an appropriate holey slice of ciabatta requires a wet dough, ideally with a hydration of 80% or more. For flavour, chewy texture, and to strengthen this wet dough, a preferment is used, and the dough is enriched with a generous amount of olive oil, which adds to the flavour. The characteristic shape and floury wrinkled surface comes from the shaping and final proving of the bread, top side down.

Although it might be possible to knead this very wet dough, working on an unfloured worktop, using the dough scraper to help stretch and fold the dough, it is not really necessary. With the preferment, and a slow rise of the main dough, one may not need to work the dough at all. I generally fold the dough in the bowl several times during the first hour and a half, then leave it to become light and airy for the rest of the fermentation time. The dough should then be handled gently, carefully deflating any particularly large holes that may have developed, but generally trying to keep as much gas in the dough as possible. The dough will tend to flatten out when tipped onto the worktop, but it will rise well in the hot oven. I generally make loaves of ciabatta, but rustic rolls can also be made just as easily, by simply dividing the dough into smaller pieces when shaping.

Method

The method for this ciabatta is somewhat different from the other preferments in this chapter, as it is not kneaded, but merely folded in the mixing bowl. Unlike the general method I use for most breads, the yeast and salt are added to the dough at the same stage, although I do not add them together, but mix one in first before adding the other.

- Combine the preferment ingredients in a bowl and mix well.
- Cover and leave to ferment for around 10 to 12 hours.
- Place the dough ingredients in a bowl and add the preferment.
- Mix well to form a wet dough.
- Drizzle a little additional olive oil over the dough, turning to coat, to help prevent sticking.
- Cover and leave to ferment for a good 3 hours.
- Fold the dough in the bowl three times, at 30 minute intervals.
- Heavily flour the worktop and tip out the dough as gently as possible, using a dough scraper to avoid tearing.
- Sprinkle the top of the dough with plenty of flour and form up into an approximately rectangular shape.
- Use the dough scraper to divide into loaves.
- Cover and allow to rise for a further 30 to 60 minutes.

- Meanwhile, heat the oven to 250°C, preferably with a baking stone, or otherwise a heavy baking sheet. Place a heavy pan at the bottom of the oven.

- Turn the loaves over so that the side resting on the worktop becomes the top of the loaf. Use a peel or the reverse side of a baking sheet to transfer the loaves to the oven.

- Add a splash of water to the pan to generate steam and bake for ten minutes before opening the oven door to allow excess steam to escape.

- Reduce the temperature to 220°C and bake for a further ten minutes or so, until the crust is golden.

Table 7.5: Ciabatta

Ingredient	g	%	Notes
preferment			
white wheat flour	200	40	
water	160	32	
yeast	0.7	0.14	
dough			
white wheat flour	300	60	
water	240	48	
olive oil	50	10	
salt	10	2	
yeast	3	0.6	
batch size (two loaves)	964	192.74	
overall formula			
white wheat flour	500	100	
water	400	80	
olive oil	50	10	
salt	10	2	
yeast	3.7	0.74	

Folding the ciabatta dough

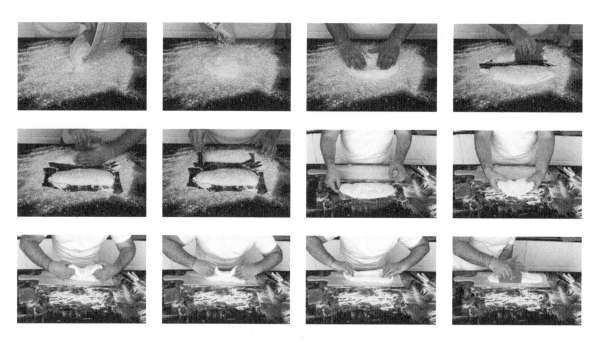

Shaping the ciabatta loaves

Ciabatta

98

7.7 Fougasse

Fougasse is the French equivalent of the Italian focaccia. Those we found some years ago in a Corsican bakery are amongst the best breads I have ever tasted, and this homemade version is likewise one of our favourites. Although some recipes for fougasse use a straight dough, and others still use a sourdough culture, I like this version with a yeasted preferment. The dough is enriched with olive oil, and develops a robust golden crust and delicious interior. Fougasse can be served plain, but can also be flavoured with herbs, olives, sundried tomatoes, or anything else the imagination might conjure. I most often make mine with a selection of good quality black and green olives. Choose those sold whole in oil, removing any stones as needed. Large olives can be split in half, but it is best to keep them in good sized pieces. It will be a little tricky to mix these in, but persist and they will go. Olives or other flavourings may be added at the end of kneading or just before shaping. Having tried both ways, I tend to prefer the latter. Fougasse can be shaped in various ways, but is characteristically slashed to form a lattice, the classic shape resembling a leaf.

Olive fougasse

Method

Initially, develop the dough as per the baguette recipe of Section 7.2, excluding the olives, if using, then proceed as follows:

- Let the dough ferment for two to three hours, folding twice, at 30 minutes intervals.
- Remove any stones from the olives, then gently work them into the dough.
- Lightly flour the worktop, tip out the dough, and then flour the top.
- Divide into portions, then stretch out the dough to form a rustic leaf shape.
- Make decorative slashes through each leaf shaped piece of dough using a dough scraper or knife, and open these slashes to form a lattice.
- Transfer the dough to baking sheets generously floured with semolina, sprinkle with a little more flour, and cover with a cloth.
- Leave to prove for another 30 to 60 minutes.
- Meanwhile, heat the oven to 250°C. Place a heavy pan at the bottom of the oven.
- Bake each fougasse individually. Transfer the baking sheet to the oven. Add a splash of water to the pan to generate steam and bake for ten minutes before opening the oven door to allow excess steam to escape.
- Reduce the temperature to 220°C and bake for a further ten to 15 minutes, until the crust is a rich golden colour.

Shaping the fougasse

Ingredient	g	%	Notes
preferment			
white wheat flour	200	29	
water	200	29	
yeast	0.7	0.1	
dough			
white wheat flour	500	71	
water	269	38	
olive oil	70	10	
salt	14	2	
yeast	4.6	0.65	
herbes de Provence (optional)	1.5 (2 tsp)	0.21	
black and green olives (optional)	250	36	
batch size (two fougasse)	*1510*	*216*	
overall formula			
white wheat flour	**700**	**100**	
water	**469**	**67**	
olive oil	**70**	**10**	
salt	**14**	**2**	
yeast	**5.3**	**0.75**	
herbes de Provence (optional)	**1.5 (2 tsp)**	**0.21**	
black and green olives (optional)	**250**	**36**	

7.8 Honey, fig, and walnut loaf

With a dozen ingredients, this bread diverges furthest from the basic formula of flour, water, yeast, and salt. However, I was keen to include a recipe with fruit and nuts. This bread is excellent with aged hard cheeses, the sweetness of the figs and honey works well with terrines, or it can be enjoyed on its own, or toasted and slathered in butter. At its heart is a one third wholemeal loaf, somewhat like the half wholemeal bread of Section 5.2. This recipe benefits, though, from a preferment of part of the white flour.

Figs and walnuts are something of a classic combination, and not uncommon in bread recipes. They are paired here with honey and, for a hint of spice, some cinnamon and cumin. At the levels suggested the spices provide a background flavour, rather than being prominent, but one can adjust to taste. Other dried fruits, such as raisins, dates, and apricots, are suitable alternatives to the figs, as are hazelnuts, almonds, and pecans, to the nuts. However, figs and walnuts are ideal; the soft figs turn jammy and the walnuts toast as the bread cooks, infusing it with great aroma and flavour. Unlike the complexities of making a bread with whole grains and seeds, the additions to this loaf do not unduly affect the development of the dough. The honey and spices can be added to the flour, and the figs and walnuts can be gently folded into the kneaded dough, being careful not to crush them. Select a soft dried fig and chop both figs and walnuts quite coarsely, so that distinct pieces will be found in the finished bread; I cut the figs into quarters and break walnut halves into two or three pieces. With most breads, I like to minimise the kneading and fold the dough several times during fermentation. Although it can be folded, it is somewhat awkward and inconvenient due to the fruit and nuts, so with this dough, it is arguably better to develop the gluten more fully during kneading instead. The recipe produces a loaf with a fairly large proportion of fruit and nuts. This is how I like it, but one may vary the proportions according to taste.

Method

Development of the dough is not much different from before, but take particular note of the following steps during preparation:

- Place the milk and butter in a pan, and raise the temperature to 85°C. If a thermometer is not available, heat until small bubbles rise, but before coming to a full boil.

- Remove from the heat, and allow to cool until lukewarm, then stir in the honey.

- Place the flour, yeast, and spices in a bowl and then add the milk mixture and the preferment.

- Mix well, then cover and leave to stand for 20 minutes.

- Continue to develop the dough as usual, kneading, resting, adding the salt, and kneading again.

- Once the dough is supple and elastic, spread out and gently fold in the chopped figs and walnuts until uniformly distributed.

- Ferment, shape, and prove, as per the preceding recipes, but do not fold during fermentation.

- As the bread contains honey and to a lesser extent milk sugars, the crust will develop a good colour, so to avoid an overly dark crust, bake entirely at 200°C for around 45 minutes. A lower internal temperature of around 88 to 90°C is appropriate for this loaf.

Table 7.7: Honey, fig, and walnut loaf

Ingredient	g	%	Notes
preferment			
white wheat flour	125	33	
water	125	33	
yeast	0.4	0.11	
dough			
white wheat flour	125	34	
wholemeal wheat flour	125	33	
milk	150	40	
butter	38	10	
honey	38	10	
chopped walnuts	100	27	
chopped figs	150	40	
ground cinnamon	4 (2 tsp)	1.1	
ground cumin	2 (1 tsp)	0.5	
salt	8	2	
yeast	1.9	0.5	
batch size (one large loaf)	992	264.21	
overall formula			
white wheat flour	250	67	
wholemeal wheat flour	125	33	
water	125	33	
milk	150	40	
butter	38	10	
honey	38	10	
chopped walnuts	100	27	
chopped figs	150	40	
ground cinnamon	4	1.1	
ground cumin	2	0.5	
salt	8	2	
yeast	2.3	0.61	

Honey, fig, and walnut loaf

8.   Sourdough

For depth of flavour, open crumb, chewy texture, and great crust, a good sourdough is hard to beat. Sourdough, known as *levain* by the French, is made using a starter culture colonised by wild yeasts and bacteria. It is the presence of the bacteria, notably *Lactobacilli*, that develops the characteristic sour flavour, although the degree of sourness can be controlled to some extent by the method of preparation. To read some authors, one might acquire the impression that breads made using baker's yeast are in some way inferior to sourdough. In my view, this would not be entirely fair, and some of my favourite white breads, such as focaccia, ciabatta, fougasse, and baguette, are made, typically, with baker's yeast. A crusty white bread, made with a preferment and a well hydrated dough, and given a proper fermentation, will also develop a nice open crumb and good chewy texture. The flavour will be excellent, but different, without the distinctive sourness of a wild yeast culture. One may well favour one or the other, but one could not reasonably say that one was better than the other.

Sourdough makes excellent white bread, but it is with dark breads, and especially those made with rye flour, that sourdough really excels. The composition of rye flour is quite different from wheat, and the acidity of the sourdough culture is beneficial with doughs made with a high proportion of rye, helping, for example, to curtail the activity of the amylase that is often present in undesirably large amounts in rye flour.

Working with sourdough is not much different from preparing bread using a preferment made with baker's yeast, albeit a slower process and without further additions of yeast. The dough proves for a long time, usually in a bowl or basket of some sort to maintain its form. Results will depend largely on the properties of the starter. If it is not sufficiently active, rise times will be unduly long and the dough too relaxed to hold its shape well when turned out for baking. A common complaint is slack doughs that spread out thinly and have poor oven bounce. With a good starter, though, the rise will be quite effective.

Many of the breads of previous sections can be adapted to a sourdough formula. Recipes vary, but a good starting point is to use an amount of starter that provides between 25 and 40% of the total flour weight. All of the recipes in this section are based on a starter prepared with equal amounts, by weight, of flour and water.

8.1   Developing and maintaining a sourdough culture

Different authors provide quite diverse instructions on developing and maintaining a sourdough culture or starter. Some authors suggest adding a little grated apple, a few chopped grapes, or similar, for the natural yeasts carried on their skins. This works well, but a starter can be made with nothing but flour and water. Organic produce is much preferred for anything to be added to a starter, whether beginning with a little fruit, or just using flour. Filtered water may also be beneficial.

I maintain one starter culture, for which I generally use a white wheat flour. Rye is often included in starters, but I prefer the structure and aroma of a starter made just with wheat. One can, of course, maintain more than one culture for different purposes. Generally, though, one prepared with white wheat, or even with a little rye in the mix, should be fine for the casual home baker. By all means experiment with different flours, which tend to develop different flavours. I would not be concerned about adding a little rye or wholemeal wheat flour to the starter and using this for a white bread, as I rarely make a white sourdough with 100% white flour, finding the addition of a little rye or wholemeal wheat flour beneficial for the flavour. If a rye starter is desired, one can add a little of a white wheat based culture to some rye and, after a couple of feeds with further rye, the proportion of white flour remaining will be insignificant.

For the initial development of a new culture, it is often suggested that one should begin with a wholemeal flour. The bran — the tough outer skin of the grain that is removed to make white flour — is particularly likely to harbour reasonable amounts of the wild yeasts we desire in the culture. I have not had, though, any trouble starting with organic white wheat flour.

Advice varies as to how much culture to maintain, the ratio of flour to water, and how to prepare it for use. After a number of starters of varying quality, this is my preferred method, which I have found to produce a reliably active starter that will readily raise a loaf in five or six hours at room temperature. Of course, the easiest way to develop a starter culture is to take a small amount of an existing culture, which can be fed up and ready for use in just a few days.

To develop a new starter I maintain about 400 g of starter culture, composed of an equal amount of flour and water by weight. This seems to me a suitable amount for general home use and enough volume to easily maintain. The quantities can be readily scaled up if needed. A kilner jar is ideal for storing the starter; allow for two to three times the volume of the culture to cater for expansion during fermentation. For the quantities suggested here a one litre jar is suitable.

- Add 100 g flour and 100 g water to a bowl or jar. Mix well, cover, and leave at room temperature for 36 to 48 hours.
- There should now be signs of life: some bubbles and an interesting aroma.
- Add 100 g flour and 100 g water, mix well, and leave for 24 hours.
- The culture should expand as fermentation gasses are produced.
- Give the culture a quick stir, then remove 200 g and discard. Add 100 g flour and 100 g water and mix well.
- Repeat daily until highly active. The starter should bubble up and expand to double the volume over the course of a few hours after feeding.

To feed Feeding simply involves removing 200 g of the starter culture, adding 100 g flour and 100 g water, and mixing well. Feeding is necessary to provide a continual source of food

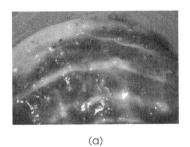

(a)   (b)   (c)   (d)

Development of a sourdough culture: (a) signs of life after 36 hours—small bubbles and distinctive aroma, (b) after first feed, (c) twelve hours after feeding—significant rise in the culture, and (d) domed top and bubbly surface characteristic of a ripe culture.

for the yeasts and bacteria, and is ideally carried out every day, but missing a day or two will not matter too much, in my experience, so long as it is properly active when needed for baking. If baking every day, one would use the portion of the culture removed during feeding to make the day's bread, but for less frequent use, it may be necessary to discard this portion of the culture. If it is not needed for a while, the culture is best stored in the refrigerator, which will slow the feeding of the yeasts. This should keep it in good condition for a week or two. Remove every week or so, allow to return to room temperature, feed, then return to the refrigerator. Remove a couple of days before needed for baking, so that it can be fed a few times to become active once again.

Preparing a starter for use The older the culture, or the more old material in the culture, the more sour the end result is likely to be. How much of this sour flavour is desired is rather a matter of individual taste. An old culture, though, will be less active and rise times may be excessive. To make sure the culture is highly active, two days before use, give it a quick stir, then remove 350 g, which will leave just a little on the bottom and around the edges of the jar. Feed with 175 g flour and 175 g water. The day before use, feed as usual.

If a large amount of starter is needed for baking, the day before, remove 50 to 100 g of the culture, place in a bowl, and add a suitable amount of flour and water according to the recipe(s) and leave for around 12 hours, ideally overnight, to develop. For example, if the recipe in question calls for 400 g of starter, add 175 g flour and 175 g water to an initial 50 g of culture.

If something goes wrong Most problems with a sourdough culture can be addressed by discarding most of it, leaving just a little on the bottom of the jar or bowl, and giving it a good feed. If the culture fails to develop properly, so that it is not particularly active, then discard and start again. Generally, though, the starter cultures are easy to maintain and quite forgiving of lapses in attention. They should not be mouldy, nor should they have a nasty smell; in either case, discard and begin again. A strong, somewhat beery and acidic aroma is to be expected, but this should not be unpleasant. It is fairly easy, by refrigerating when not in use, to keep a starter culture healthy for months without any problems. Some sourdough bakeries have starter cultures that have been kept going for decades.

8.2   The schedule

Aside from the maintenance of the starter, the process does not require more effort than a bread made with baker's yeast and a preferment. It may, though, require a little more time. This does depend on the temperature and how active the starter is, but, at normal room temperature, I would expect rise times of two to four times that of those recipes I prepare with baker's yeast. For me, this dictates one of two convenient schedules. Most often I will prepare the starter late evening, either refreshing the existing culture, or, if making a larger batch of bread, taking a portion of it and adding to a larger batch of flour and water to develop overnight. I then prepare the dough in the morning, typically between 8:00 and 10:00. I use the same slow process to develop the dough as for the previous recipes, taking about one hour, after which it ferments for around two hours before being divided, if necessary, and shaped. With my starter culture and at our typical kitchen temperature, the final prove generally takes from four to eight hours, with five hours being fairly typical. Starting at 8:00, then, I would typically expect to be getting the loaves in the oven from 16:00 to 17:00, in good time for dinner.

The alternative is to prove the loaves overnight. This means preparing the starter in the morning, shaping the loaves as late as possible in the evening, and baking off in the morning. The one difficulty with this schedule is that the dough may be over proved by morning. One can find a cool place for the dough to prove to slow the process, reduce the amount of starter in the recipe, or retard the dough in the refrigerator and finish the proving at room temperature the next day. Some experiment may be needed to find a schedule that works under the given conditions.

8.3   Shaping, proving, and baking

Shaping sourdough is essentially the same as for any of the previous recipes. Although the initial fermentation is not usually that much longer, the final prove tends to take a long time. With my starter and method I generally expect it to take around five hours, but it can be eight hours or so. Forming a boule or batard, and leaving to prove on a baking sheet, the dough would relax quite considerably during proving, and it is all too easy to produce a pancake rather than a loaf. Hence, all of these sourdough loaves are proved in bannetons — cane baskets that are available in various shapes and sizes. The bannetons hold the dough in a suitable shape during the prove. They should be floured generously before use, wholemeal rye flour being ideal and far more effective than wheat flour, allowing even fairly high hydration doughs to be removed without any sticking.

Deciding the ideal moment to bake can be challenging with sourdough. With a dough prepared with baker's yeast, the rise and proving times are fairly consistent, and can be quite predictable if the amount of yeast, and the dough, fermentation, and proving temperatures, are controlled. Such doughs will generally double in size without difficulty and one can depress the dough with a finger and observe its response to judge whether it is under proved, over proved, or just right, as described in Section 4.7. With sourdough it is a little more difficult, as the dough tends to be more relaxed from the lengthy prove and it is much less clear when it is ready. It may not rise quite as much as the doughs of the previous chapters, and may be ready when increased by only half as much in volume. Unlike baker's yeast, the behaviour of the sourdough culture is less predictable, some being more vigorous than others, and varying also according to the feeding regime. In this area, practice and experiment will be needed to become comfortable with the habits of the dough for the given starter culture. It is best to err on the side of under proved, as over proved dough responds poorly in the oven.

For baking, the loaf is tipped from the banneton directly onto a peel, where it is scored and then loaded into the oven. A baking stone is certainly to be recommended. A popular alternative is the cast iron Dutch oven or a purpose made clay baking dome. These are first heated in the oven, then taken out and the lids removed. A light sprinkling of coarse flour may be applied to the base, then the dough is tipped from the banneton straight into the hot dish, quickly scored, if desired, then the lid put back on and the whole thing returned to the oven. Within the enclosed environment, the steam released by the baking dough serves the same purpose as the steam one otherwise attempts to introduce at the start of the bake. The bread is baked with the lid on for around two thirds of the time, then the lid is removed, allowing the crust to dry and brown properly.

Sourdough loaves proving in bannetons

The bannetons I use are sized at 250 g / ½ lb, 500 g / 1 lb, and 1 kg / 2 lb. Baking times will vary, of course, with loaf size. I bake these breads according to the usual schedule: heating the oven to 250°C for around one hour before baking, with a baking stone — or baking dome or heavy baking sheet — and a heavy pan in the bottom of the oven; turning out, scoring, and loading the loaf as quickly as possible; adding a cup of hot water to the pan to generate some steam; baking for ten minutes; opening the oven door to allow excess steam to escape and turning the oven down to 220°C; and then baking for a further ten to 15 minutes for a 250 g loaf, 20 to 30 minutes for a 500 g loaf, and 25 to 35 minutes for a 1 kg loaf. One might extend the bake somewhat if using a Dutch oven or baking dome, perhaps 40 to 50 minutes for a 1 kg loaf. Ovens vary, so it is useful to check the internal temperature of the bread for as least the first few bakes until one is comfortable with the timings. For these recipes, I like to achieve an internal temperature of around 98 to 99°C.

8.4 White sourdough

This recipe is the sourdough equivalent of the basic white dough of Section 5.1. The quantities are identical, except this time 200 g of flour and 200 g of water are contributed by the sourdough starter, comprising a little over one third of the total flour content. I usually prepare the starter the evening before, adding, say, 50 g of existing sourdough culture to 175 g flour and 175 g water to make the required 400 g total. As before, I like to add a little wholemeal rye flour to this otherwise white wheat dough. This contributes flavour, texture, and colour to the bread, without having any noticeable detrimental effect on the density of the loaf.

Table 8.1: White sourdough

Ingredient	g	%	Notes
starter			
white wheat flour	200	36	
water	200	36	
dough			
white wheat flour	295	54	
wholemeal rye flour	55	10	
water	185	34	
salt	11	2	
batch size (1 kg or 2 × 500 g bannetons)	*946*	*172*	
overall formula			
white wheat flour	**495**	**90**	
wholemeal rye flour	**55**	**10**	
water	**385**	**70**	
salt	**11**	**2**	

Method

The general approach to developing the dough is essentially the same as for those recipes based on preferments described in the previous chapter:

- Prepare the sourdough starter 12 hours before use.
- Place the dough ingredients, except for the salt, in a bowl and add the starter.
- Mix well then cover and leave to stand for 20 minutes.

- Tip the dough out onto the worktop and knead for a few minutes, until the dough starts to come together.

- Turn over the bowl to cover the dough and leave for ten minutes or so.

- Spread the dough a little, and sprinkle over the salt.

- Fold and work the dough to incorporate the salt, then continue to knead until fairly smooth and elastic.

- Form the dough into a ball, using a little flour if needed.

- Lightly flour the bowl, return the dough to the bowl, and cover with a cloth.

- Let the dough ferment for two to three hours, folding the dough three times at 30 minute intervals.

- Lightly flour the worktop and tip out the dough.

- Divide into portions as needed, gently degas, and shape to suit the banneton(s) to be used.

- Flour the banneton(s) generously with wholemeal rye flour and place in the dough, seam side up.

- Cover and allow to prove for around four to eight hours. The dough may not quite double in size, so be careful not to over prove.

- One hour before baking, heat the oven to 250°C, preferably with a baking stone, or otherwise a heavy baking sheet. Place a heavy pan at the bottom of the oven.

- Flour a peel or the reverse side of a baking sheet with semolina or rye flour and gently turn out the loaf from the banneton.

- Use a sharp blade to score the loaf and then transfer to the oven.

- Add a splash of water to the pan to generate steam and bake for ten minutes before opening the oven door to allow excess steam to escape.

- Reduce the temperature to 220°C and bake according to the size of the banneton(s) used, as described in Section 8.3.

8.5 Sourdough pain de campagne

This is a sourdough version of the pain de campagne recipe of Section 7.3, which was prepared with a preferment using baker's yeast. It is a good all round sourdough recipe, with plenty of flavour coming from the wholemeal wheat and rye, but without too dense a texture that higher proportions of wholemeal flours would bring. It is, perhaps, similar to the German *Landbrot*. The hydration is increased over the white dough, above, to counter the higher absorption of the wholemeal flours, resulting in a similarly open crumb. For the method, refer to the white sourdough of Section 8.4.

White sourdough (top), sourdough pain de campagne (bottom)

Table 8.2: Sourdough pain de campagne

Ingredient	g	%	Notes
starter			
white wheat flour	200	33	
water	200	33	
dough			
white wheat flour	220	37	
wholemeal wheat flour	90	15	
wholemeal rye flour	90	15	
water	240	40	
salt	12	2	
batch size (1 kg or 2 × 500 g bannetons)	*1052*	*175*	
overall formula			
white wheat flour	420	70	
wholemeal wheat flour	90	15	
wholemeal rye flour	90	15	
water	440	73	
salt	12	2	

8.6 Wholemeal wheat and rye sourdough

This is one of my favourite sourdough recipes. With 58% of the flour being wholemeal wheat and rye, it is a moderately dark bread, of a similar nature to many of the eastern and northern European breads. The crumb is closer than that of the pain de campagne, but not unduly dense. With this recipe, I like to include a little honey; not so much that the result is particularly sweet, but for flavour and to provide some balance with the acidity of the sourdough culture, but it is optional and can be omitted if preferred. For the method, refer to the white sourdough of Section 8.4.

8.7 Spelt sourdough

This recipe is essentially a sourdough equivalent of the spelt bread of Section 5.4. The crumb is less open than the white sourdough or pain de campagne, but still reasonably light, especially for a wholemeal loaf, thanks to the high hydration, without which it would be rather heavy. One can lighten it further, if desired, by using some white spelt flour, where available, or by substituting white wheat flour if preferred, with a reduction in the hydration to suit.

As I usually maintain only a white wheat sourdough culture, I add a little of this to spelt flour and water, around 12 hours before preparing the main dough, to make a spelt starter for this bread, which is why the recipe has 4% white wheat flour. For the method, refer to the white sourdough of Section 8.4.

Table 8.3: Wholemeal wheat and rye sourdough

Ingredient	g	%	Notes
starter			
white wheat flour	145	29	
water	145	29	
dough			
white wheat flour	65	13	
wholemeal wheat flour	145	29	
wholemeal rye flour	145	29	
water	225	45	
butter	25	5	
honey	40	8	
salt	10	2	
batch size (1 kg or 2 × 500 g bannetons)	*945*	*189*	
overall formula			
white wheat flour	**210**	**42**	
wholemeal wheat flour	**145**	**29**	
wholemeal rye flour	**145**	**29**	
water	**370**	**74**	
butter	**25**	**5**	
honey	**40**	**8**	
salt	**10**	**2**	

Table 8.4: Spelt sourdough

Ingredient	g	%	Notes
starter			
white wheat flour	25	4	
water	25	4	
spelt starter			
wholemeal spelt flour	175	32	
water	175	32	
dough			
wholemeal spelt flour	350	64	
water	215	39	
salt	11	2	
batch size (1 kg or 2 × 500 g bannetons)	*976*	*177*	
overall formula			
wholemeal spelt flour	**525**	**96**	
white wheat flour	**25**	**4**	
water	**415**	**75**	
salt	**11**	**2**	

Wholemeal wheat and rye (top), spelt sourdough (bottom)

8.8 Rye sourdough

This is an almost 100% rye sourdough and has the dark, dense, sour flavour typical of such breads. It may not be to everyone's taste, but with family from Finland, I have become rather fond of the full flavour of this sort of bread. As with the spelt sourdough above, I begin by making a rye starter, adding a little of my white wheat culture to rye flour and water. The small amount of wheat has no discernible effect on the dough. If one maintains a rye starter, though, this can be used instead.

I often add a little honey to this sort of bread, which brings a further dimension to the flavour, without making it particularly sweet. It is optional, and the bread is good with or without, so I include it, or not, on a whim.

When working with doughs with high proportions of rye flour, kneading is replaced by gentle mixing. There is insufficient gluten, so no benefit in kneading, whilst the starches that form much of the structure of a rye bread are easily damaged by overworking. The dough cannot be shaped in the usual way either, so is just formed into a rough ball and placed in the banneton to ferment.

Table 8.5: Rye sourdough

Ingredient	g	%	Notes
starter			
white wheat flour	25	4	
water	25	4	
rye starter			
wholemeal rye flour	200	35	
water	200	35	
dough			
wholemeal rye flour	350	61	
water	250	44	
honey (optional)	46	8	
salt	11	2	
batch size (1 kg or 2 × 500 g bannetons)	*1107*	*193*	
overall formula			
wholemeal rye flour	**550**	**96**	
white wheat flour	**25**	**4**	
water (optional)	**475**	**83**	
honey	**46**	**8**	
salt	**11**	**2**	

Method

- Place the ingredients for the rye starter in a bowl and add the white wheat starter.
- Mix well, then cover and allow to ferment for around 12 hours.
- Place all of the dough ingredients into a bowl, add the rye starter, and mix well.
- Cover and allow to rest for 30 minutes.
- Lightly dust the worktop with flour.
- Scoop out the dough, divide as needed, and form each portion into a rough ball, making sure it is well floured.
- Generously flour the banneton(s) with more rye flour.
- Place the dough into the banneton(s) and cover.
- Allow to ferment for 8 to 10 hours.
- Bake following the usual schedule.

Rye sourdough

Lightning Source UK Ltd.
Milton Keynes UK
UKOW07f0621151015

260592UK00002B/7/P